SALAH

SALAH

Updated Edition

LUCA CAIOLI
&
CYRIL COLLOT

ICON

First published in the UK in 2019
by Icon Books Ltd, Omnibus Business Centre,
39–41 North Road, London N7 9DP
email: info@iconbooks.com
www.iconbooks.com

This updated edition published in the UK in 2020

Sold in the UK, Europe and Asia
by Faber & Faber Ltd, Bloomsbury House,
74–77 Great Russell Street,
London WC1B 3DA or their agents

Distributed in the UK, Europe and Asia
by Grantham Book Services,
Trent Road, Grantham NG31 7XQ

Distributed in the USA
by Publishers Group West,
1700 Fourth Street, Berkeley, CA 94710

Distributed in Australia and New Zealand
by Allen & Unwin Pty Ltd,
PO Box 8500, 83 Alexander Street,
Crows Nest, NSW 2065

Distributed in South Africa
by Jonathan Ball, Office B4, The District,
41 Sir Lowry Road, Woodstock 7925

Distributed in India by Penguin Books India,
7th Floor, Infinity Tower – C, DLF Cyber City,
Gurgaon 122002, Haryana

Distributed in Canada by Publishers Group Canada,
76 Stafford Street, Unit 300
Toronto, Ontario M6J 2S1

ISBN: 978-1-78578-677-8

Typeset in New Baskerville by Marie Doherty

Printed and bound in Great Britain by Clays Ltd, Elcograf S.p.A.

About the authors

Luca Caioli is the bestselling author of *Messi, Ronaldo, Neymar* and *Mbappé*. A renowned Italian sports journalist, he lives in Spain.

Cyril Collot is a French sports journalist. He is the author of several books and documentaries about French football, and the bestselling biographies *Griezmann, Pogba* and *Martial*.

About the Authors

Contents

Chapter 1
Quite a history

It was all the fault of the pharaohs and the English.

Take Amenhotep II, seventh monarch of the eighteenth dynasty. An inscription on the Stele of Archery, discovered near the Sphinx, reads: 'he mastered horse riding and there was no one like him […] His bow could not be bent by anyone and no one could catch him in the races.' That was not all: it was also said of the sovereign – who reigned over Egypt from 1427 to 1401 BC – that he could handle a 30-foot long oar. Quite an undertaking.

Amenhotep II was not the only athlete pharaoh.

Take Ramesses II (1279–13 BC), one of the most powerful and famous rulers. On the obelisk in Rome's Piazza del Popolo, he is described as 'Lord of the Panegirie', a Greek word used to refer to athletic contests in Ancient Egypt. He is said to have been an impeccable archer, who was skilled at chariot racing, rode camels and horses and was unbeatable at swordsmanship.

Were these isolated cases? No. All rulers, including Hatshepsut, the second female pharaoh (1479–57 BC), had to complete a three-lap race around two ritual constructions. For many the ceremony represented a primitive Olympics, for others a symbolic rite of rejuvenation for the pharaoh, who justified his or her power in front of courtiers and the gods. The event was held every three years from the 30th year of their reign. It may not have been an Olympiad in the modern sense, but it does demonstrate how important athletic prowess was both for demigods such as the pharaohs and for young Egyptians needing to temper their physique and character.

Wrestling, boxing, horse riding, archery, running, long jump, high jump, javelin throwing, weightlifting, fencing with poles and sticks, swimming and rowing were the most popular and widely practised disciplines. There were precise rules of competition, 'sports facilities' built ad hoc, impartial referees, or at least proclaimed as such, and different coloured uniforms to distinguish the teams. The winners were rewarded with large collars that covered their chest and shoulders. Even the losers were recognised for their competitive spirit in a style worthy of Pierre de Coubertin. See, for example, the report of a race, there and back, between the Royal Palace of Memphis and the Faiyum Oasis, held in the sixth year of the reign of the Pharaoh Taharqa (690–667 BC). The stele erected to commemorate the event recalls that the ruler personally accompanied the race on his chariot, through the desert and, after the race, 'distinguished the first among them to arrive and arranged for him to eat and drink with his bodyguards. He distinguished those others who were just behind him and rewarded them with all manner of things.'

Ball games deserve a chapter in their own right. Many different kinds of balls have been discovered in Egyptian tombs. Made of wood, clay and leather, stitched and filled with straw, strips of papyrus or pressed palm leaves. With diameters ranging from three to nine centimetres, these also included coloured balls and some that were extremely heavy. Yet they are seemingly handled with ease by the figures in the painting in the main chamber of the tomb of the Governor Baqet III (circa 2000 BC) in the necropolis of Beni

Hasan to the south of Cairo. Four girls, two on the shoulders of their partners, are depicted throwing and catching spheres. It was a pastime that seems to have been reserved for, or at least favoured by women. Boys preferred to hit a ball with a palm stick, similar in shape to the ones used in modern day field hockey. But this was not merely a game for young people. During the eighteenth dynasty, under the reign of Thutmose III (1481–25 BC), one of the great leaders and strategists of Egyptian history, a ritual came into being and was documented on the walls of the Temple of Deir el-Bahari: in the presence of a deity (usually Hathor), the king hits the ball with a stick, symbolically destroying the devil's eye of the serpent god Apophis.

Speaking of balls ... Herodotus of Halicarnassus, the Greek historian who travelled along the Nile in around 450 BC, described the scene of a group of young men kicking a ball made of goatskin and straw in the second book of his *Histories* (Euterpe). In short, as was true of many other ancient civilisations – from China to Japan, from Imperial Rome to the peoples of Mesoamerica – playing with a ball was both ritual and entertainment in the Egypt of the pharaohs. But it was the British who turned a game played for centuries and centuries into a sport. They formalised it, dictated its rules, stamped it with the label 'football' and exported it all over the world. In 1863, thirteen delegates from clubs in England and Scotland met at the Freemasons' Tavern in London to found the Football Association and to set down the laws of the world's most popular sport in black and white. Nineteen years later, the British invaded Egypt in support of the Khedivate to counter the rise of nationalism, thereby gaining control of the Suez Canal, a maritime route vital to the British Empire. They exported their game, their rules and their customs. Football arrived with the occupying troops. The British soldiers built pitches and set up goals on their bases. The Egyptians looked at them strangely at first – as was the case more or less everywhere – dismissing them as mad Englishmen. They collapsed into fits of laughter when they saw the soldiers in shorts running around after a ball. But things changed quickly and puzzled looks soon turned into imitation. Football spread like wildfire from the cities. The first Egyptian team was formed in 1883, principally of players from Cairo, under the leadership of its captain Mohamed Effendi Nashed. They challenged the British, their masters and mentors, winning on several occasions – at least according to Egyptian reports, which add, perhaps with more than a touch of nationalism, that Nashed's eleven beat their foreign occupiers, at least symbolically. Nine years on football experienced a boom. In 1892, physical education in schools became compulsory, a decision that led to the formation of a great many football teams.

The dawn of the 20th century saw the birth of the country's great clubs. The Al Ahly club was founded as a sports club for Cairo's students on 24 April 1907. Its first president was Englishman Michael Inse. On 5 January 1911, also in the capital, a Belgian lawyer George Marzbach founded Qasr Al-Nil, a club for non-British expatriates. The club was open to everyone, Egyptians and foreigners; no one was excluded for ethnic, economic or social reasons. In 1952, after several changes of name, it became known definitively after the district that occupies the northern part of the island of Gezira: Zamalek.

Al Ahly and Zamalek, the two teams that have dominated Egyptian and African football ever since. Thirty-nine league titles, 36 Egypt Cups and twenty international trophies for the Red Devils of Al Ahly; twelve league titles, 25 Egypt Cups and five African Champions Leagues for the White Nights of

Zamalek. Derbies at the Cairo International Stadium have been known to attract up to 100,000 spectators.

But let's go back to the early years of the last century. On 11 September 1916, representatives of the British forces and the Egyptian clubs met in Cairo to form the EEFA, the Egyptian-English Football Association. The first official competition was held that same year: the Sultani Cup, under the patronage of Sultan Hussein Kamel, was open to British and local teams. The British won the first five editions, a domination interrupted in the 1921–22 season by the club that would go on to become Zamalek.

On 21 May 1923, Egypt was the first Arab nation and the first African country to join FIFA. This is not its only record. It was also the first African nation to participate in an Olympics, in Belgium in 1920, when its team lost 2–1 to Italy in the qualifying round in Ghent; it was also the first to play in a World Cup, in Italy in 1934, where it lost 4–2 in its opening game against Hungary, but gave birth to the first star of African football: Abdulrahman Fawzi, who scored two goals for the Pharaohs. It would also be the first country to win the Africa Cup of Nations in 1957. Egypt beat Ethiopia in the final 4–0, with a brace from El-Diba, who scored all four goals and became the top scorer with a total of five throughout the competition.

Nine years later, on 22 October 1948, the first Egyptian league was played under the auspices of King Farouk I. Eleven teams took part: Al Ahly, Farouk (now Zamalek), Al Sekka Al Hadid, Tersana, Ismaily, Misri, Port Fouad, Olympic, Ittihad, Tram and Yunan. Al Ahly eventually took home the 30-kilogram silver champions trophy.

More than 70 years have passed since then. Egypt has lived through the *coup d'etat* led by Mohamed Nagib and Colonel Gamal Abdel Nasser in 1952 and the end of the reign of King Farouk I. It has suffered the Six-Day War, which, in 1967, led to the defeat of Egyptian troops and the occupation, by the Israelis, of the Sinai Peninsula and the Gaza Strip. There was also the Yom Kippur War against the State of Israel in October 1973. The entire nation saw the death of Anwar Sadat broadcast live, when the president was assassinated on 6 October 1981 during a military parade in Cairo. It suffered the 30-year government of Hosni Mubarak. It was filled with hope during the 2011 revolution of Tahrir Square and the Arab Spring. It witnessed the fall of President Mubarak and voted in the presidential elections of 2012 that gave victory to Mohamed Morsi, a candidate from the Muslim Brotherhood. It suffered another *coup d'etat* by General Abdel Fatteḥ el-Sisi, who dismissed Mohamed Morsi and was proclaimed president of the republic. It mourned the thousands of victims of the protests at the Rabaa massacre in August 2013. Abdel Fatteḥ el-Sisi now rules over the country with an iron fist and, in the presidential elections of 28 March 2018, ridiculed by many observers, obtained 97 per cent of the vote.

What about football? According to Bob Bradley, manager of the Egyptian national side from 2011 to 2013: 'When you come here, you get a real sense of how football is part of all this. You realise how football and politics are totally connected.' Football is the mirror of a complex society: an instrument used by regimes to cement loyalty and nationalism, an element of distraction from the difficulties of everyday life and a laboratory for new ideas and rebellions. In these 70 years, football has established itself as both the great passion and the great folly of the Egyptians. It has served up successes and dramas alike. Seven African Cups won by the Pharaohs national side and the Port Said riot of 1 February 2012. A postponement of the Egyptian league, matches behind closed doors and, in February 2015, before the game between Zamalek and ENPPI, yet another massacre. It has produced clubs like Al Ahly, with 50 million fans and 23,000 spectators per game, 'the African team of the twentieth century,' according to the Confederation of African Football. It has also witnessed the birth of the White Knights (UWK), the Zamalek Ultras, one of the most turbulent fringes of Egyptian fans and one of the leading groups in the 2011 uprisings. It has trained players such as Mohamed Aboutrika, the philosopher, the legend, the midfielder who delivered three African Cups for his country and has ultimately been exiled, accused of suspicious ties to the Muslim Brotherhood. Or Hossam Hassan, the Maradona of the Nile: 69 goals for his national team. Or Ahmed Hassan, with a record number of caps for his country (184, to be precise). Or even Essam el-Hadary, the oldest player to have ever played in the final stages of a World Cup (aged 45 years and 161 days), at Russia 2018; and Mido, or Ahmed Hossam Hussein Abdelhamid, the unruly genius. The latest pharaoh, the latest hero celebrated in modern Egypt, is Mohamed Salah. He is the footballer who shows the clean face of the country, the good Muslim who triumphs in the land of the former occupiers, subverting the feeling of inferiority instilled by the colonialists, the man who tells children never to stop dreaming or believing in their dreams, the symbol of hope and the collective joy for a people tired economically, politically and socially.

Chapter 2
Son of a jasmine trader

Fields of flowering jasmine to the right; green maize plants to the left. On the edge of the dirt road that cuts through the countryside, a cart pulled by a donkey is being driven by an old man with a white beard, a cream *jellabiya* and a white skullcap. A tuk-tuk speeds off quickly in a cloud of dust. And there, in the distance, the terracotta-coloured minarets and houses of Nagrig appear.

There are no signs announcing this Nile Delta village of some 15,000 inhabitants and 150 cultivated acres. Even those born nearby sometimes have to stop and ask for directions. Not to mention how long it takes to get here … Three hours to travel the 131 kilometres that separate Nagrig from Cairo. Bridges, elevated roads, clogged bypasses: getting out of the Egyptian capital is a mass of traffic and a cacophony of horns that never stops, day or night. A continuous concert in which the noise of the cars, tuk-tuks, overloaded minivans, lorries and buses merges with the gestures of drivers and pedestrians, who cross wherever they please with a simple wave of the hand to alert those behind the wheel. You can almost reach out and touch European cars from the 1960s, with German number plates on top of which Egyptian licences have been stuck haphazardly; vehicles rammed with children looking out of the windows, waving; motorbikes with four passengers and a veiled woman in the middle, holding a baby. Every now and then the Nile appears, along the Corniche. It slips away

majestically, leaving its islands behind. Advertising hoard-
ings spring up on all sides, getting bigger and bigger, more
invasive and insistent. They hide ochre towers, skyscrapers
and yet more skyscrapers, each one taller than the next in
an attempt to exceed the height of the Great Pyramid of
Giza. There is no escape from this city of more than 20 million; it follows you for miles and miles, even once you're on
the Agricultural Road to Alexandria. Houses and more red-
brick houses, unfinished, with dark, empty windows. Piles
and piles of bricks and cement bags, stacked up waiting for
the money to come in so the work can be finished. Iron
frameworks soar up and up, awaiting better times. Buildings
that have been attempted before collapsing and being left
there, monuments in the desert. Palm leaf roofs and satellite dishes; kids flying coloured kites and donkeys waiting to
be put to work. Then, little by little, the green of the fertile
land of the Nile Delta comes into view: tall palm trees in the
distance, maize and alfalfa compete for space with illegally
built houses. The train bound for Alexandria runs alongside.
A sea of passengers perches between one wagon and the
next, balancing precariously over the rails.

The motorway is lined by makeshift barbecues and ven-
dors selling chargrilled corn. They weave in between the cars
to offer their wares to the drivers. The road continues on
into the Qalyubia Governorate, the city of Banha and, after
the police checkpoints, the Monufia Governorate, the land
of presidents. Anwar Sadat and Mubarak were both born
in this region that was also originally home to the family of
Abdel Fattah el-Sisi. There are plenty of reminders of the
president: banners stuck on poles along the road, bearing
the face of the field marshal, perhaps left over from the
elections of 28 March 2018. Once past the 'triumphal arch'
of Tanta, capital of Gharbia, the road, which is bordered by

cotton plantations, becomes narrow and full of potholes. Piles of plastic waste and even a dead and bloated horse lie at the side of the road. Rubbish of all kinds invades the banks and canals of the Nile as it cross the fields. Towns and villages come one after the other, displaying themselves like an open book: women offering up fish on straw mats; horse-drawn carts flashing yellow melons and watermelons; skinned lambs attached to hooks in butchers' doorways; car dealers, where you can find everything from a chassis to an engine dismantled for parts; cafés, where only men are intent on peacefully smoking hookah pipes; narrow alleyways teeming with children. More fields and then finally the turn off for Nagrig.

You enter this *fellaheen* (peasant in Arabic) village along a dirt road, passing a cart pulled by a donkey. Towing a blotchy cow. It's being driven by a boy, fourteen at most, wearing a red and yellow shirt, a Roma shirt, stamped with the number 11 and the name M. Salah. A few hundred yards further on, the monotony of the ochre of the earth and houses, the predominant colour, is broken by a luminous green. Behind a gate, surrounded by freshly painted orange walls, a brand new artificial football pitch is bordered by floodlights.

You would never expect to find anything like this in such a remote village. Three men are lying by the touchline, watching the kids play. One of the boys, waiting for a cross from his friend, is wearing the number 10 shirt of the Egyptian national team, again printed with the name Salah. When you ask for an explanation, the adults can't agree: some say it was built by the army, others that it was Pepsi (Liverpool's sponsor) who funded it. No one is in any doubt as to why though: as a tribute to their illustrious fellow citizen, Mohamed Salah, who was born in this village on 15 June 1992.

Walking along the village's dirt roads and alleyways, where roaring motorbikes, cars, carts, cows, donkeys, horses and stray dogs live side by side, you tunnel through a spider's web of cables hanging down all over the place; you pass in front of shops selling anything and everything; of houses with colourful, gilded balconies, like opera boxes, or half-built constructions and those decorated with scenes of flora and fauna. Many have simple paintings on their façades: planes, boats, coaches and the Kaaba, reminders that the owners have fulfilled the duty of every devout Muslim, to visit Mecca at least once in their lifetime. A pilgrimage to and around the house of God that gives everyone the opportunity to ask for forgiveness for their sins, to repent and to purify themselves. Veiled women and men in Western dress or *jellabiyas* smile and wave at visitors. They are down-to-earth, friendly and helpful. Curious but not angered by the sudden popularity of Nagrig due to the rise of the Pharaoh's number 10 and Liverpool's number 11.

Before journalists and cameramen from all over the world arrived to see where Mo grew up and kicked his first football, Nagrig was known for growing red onions and the jasmine that is exported to France, Russia and Ukraine to be used in the perfume industry. And for having been the birthplace, back in 1810, when the village was still called Nagrid, of Sheikh Muhammad Ayyad al-Tantawi, who emigrated from the Nile Delta to Russia in 1840; seven years later, he became Chair of Arabic Studies at Saint Petersburg University. Ayyad al-Tantawi wrote an interesting account of the first ten years of his life spent in an immense country so different from his own. Entitled *Tuhfat al-adhkiya' bi-akhbar bilad al-Rusiya* (The Precious Gift of the Sharp-Witted in the News about the Russian Land), it offers a picture of Czarist Russia and the culture and customs of its people. He was a great scholar but not the global star Mo Salah is today. The story comes, animatedly, from the footballer's parents' neighbours.

Sitting on the porch, an elderly woman with a little girl and a man busy with a motorbike and trailer talk about the many foreigners and Egyptians who have been to see Mo and his family's home. Three storeys, grey concrete with rounded balconies like the seats on rides at a country fair; nothing special apart from the bolted gate overlooked by two CCTV cameras. They must be the only cameras in the village. Mo's family are not there, explains Um Ali, a neighbour opposite. They could be in Cairo or England, but what he does know is that they decided to escape the siege of journalists and scroungers some time ago.

The story of Mo and the land where he grew up is told by Maher Anwar, Mayor of Nagrig. He lives on the second floor of a corner house. Bags of onions hang drying up the stairs. One of his daughters answers the door; apparently her father has gone to a nearby village but will be back soon. He returns after about half an hour. The man of the house removes his shoes on the doorstep and makes his guests comfortable in the lounge: gold sofas and armchairs, floral patterned rugs and green curtains like sacred vestments. With a salt and pepper moustache, glasses with a thin frame, a white *jellabiya* and a placid, smiling face, the first citizen of Nagrig offers his visitors a drink and begins to talk.

'Mo was born to a good family. His father was a government official and one of the biggest jasmine exporters in the area. His mother worked in an office. They're a family who love football. Salah Hamed Mehrez Zaki Ghali, Mo's father, played here in the amateur team at the village youth club in the 80s and 90s. He was a good defender. His uncle wasn't bad either. Who knows, maybe that's where he got his passion from? With his brother and sister, Mo grew up happy. Like so many other Egyptian children, when he was seven or eight, he would spend hours and hours playing football in the street, on the youth club pitch or at school. When he was ten or twelve, he was fast and talented. His potential was obvious. It was spotted by Ghamry Abdel Hamid el-Saadany, one of his first coaches, and his father. They took him to El Mahalla, the largest town in the region, for a trial but Baladeyet (a second division Egyptian league club) didn't want him. He was too small and puny. He ended up at Ittihad Basyoun, the team in a village a few kilometres away. Then one day a scout came to the club and told the boys to play a match so he could watch them. He'd come to see a different boy, Sherif, but when he saw Mo he was impressed and offered him the chance to go and play for Osmanson Tanta. That's where Salah began his adventure in Egyptian then in European football.'

This is the mayor's version. Others claim Liverpool's number 10 was discovered at a school futsal tournament sponsored by Pepsi. This theory is flatly dismissed in Tanta.

Maher Anwar has other guests waiting for him. A reporter from a Swiss German daily newspaper is waiting her turn in the hall. 'Journalists come here from all over the world,' the mayor says. 'We're happy about it and we thank Salah for making our village famous across the globe.'

What do his citizens think about all this interest? 'Nagrig,' he answers calmly, 'is a village like many others in the Nile Delta, but it is characterised by the friendliness and goodness of its people.'

They don't mind that they've become a tourist destination for the international media. One last question. What does Salah represent for Nagrig? 'Hope, not just for his people but for Egypt and Africa as a whole. He's an example of how far you can go, what you can do in life with effort and passion.'

A few yards from the mayor's house, in the corner of a little square, the barber's shop is packed. With music playing in the background, the customers wait outside to get their hair and beards trimmed. Between one cut and the next, Ahmed Ramadan is happy to tell us about his friendship with Salah and their shared passion: 'We used to play football near the school. We would always challenge each other, one-on-one. We'd start playing and then other boys would join in. People would come and watch. Mohamed shone even then but there were lots of boys who were good and people would say they would go to one club or another. We both ended up at Ittihad Basyoun. Then he went on to become what he's become, but he hasn't changed. He's still a modest and simple boy, a good person.'

The barber's impression is confirmed by Mustafa: 'Whenever he comes back to Nagrig you see him on the street. He goes to the café or the mosque to pray like anyone else. He's certainly not someone who goes around with a bodyguard.'

'He plays ping pong and billiards here in the café and is happy to have selfies with the kids who ask, or to sign autographs,' says Mohamed Bassyoni, a childhood friend who remembers when he used to play with Mo and his brother Nasr. He insists on the fact that even if Salah is now a footballer who is famous around the world, he doesn't act like it and is not ashamed of his origins.

'Mohamed has stayed on the straight and narrow thanks to his family and the customs of our village. He visits neighbours and relatives for celebrations like Eid al-Fitr. He came to visit me during Ramadan to see how I was. I'd had a car accident, nothing serious. He's very attached to the village where he grew up.' The mayor remembers one example: 'Mo got married in Cairo but they celebrated here afterwards and everyone was invited. The village loves Salah because he has done and continues to do a lot for it.'

To find out more it is worth going to talk to Mohamed el-Bahnasy. In a long, narrow alleyway leading to one of the village's many mosques, he can be found behind the desk of his book and stationery shop. Hello Kitty diaries, cardboard printed with red hearts, holy books, calendars and posters of Mohamed Salah occupy the walls and shelves of the tiny shop. With a grey beard, thinning hair, a white tunic and the air of a wise old man, el-Bahnasy – in agreement with Mo's father, uncle and brother – manages 50,000 Egyptian pounds from the Mohamed Salah Charitable Foundation every month. 'It goes to widows, orphans, large families with very little support, and to the hospitals,' he says, showing a book covered in dense blue writing. It lists the names of those requesting assistance. 'We study every case and decide whether to contribute financially. But this is only a part of Salah's donations: there's a secret part he gives, as a good Muslim, but no one knows who he is helping and it has to remain a secret.' The wise old sage puts the book back down on the table, adjusts his glasses and adds: 'Given the economic situation Egyptians are suffering, we need men like Salah to help people.'

Yes, the economic situation … In June 2018, the Cairo government announced fresh cuts to electricity subsidies and steep rises in petrol and cooking gas. A few months earlier, there had been increases in drinking water prices and recent years have seen cuts to flour, bread and milk subsidies – one of the austerity measures imposed by the International Monetary Foundation in exchange for a loan of $12 billion. A neo-liberalist strategy intended to stabilise the economy and attract new investment; a policy of reforms and austerity that signified a sharp cut in wages and a severe blow to standards of living among the middle and poorest classes.

El-Bahnasy is right to repeat again and again that the help provided by the Liverpool number 11 is very important with things as they are. He says: 'Salah is a gift from Allah. With his help he has become a trader in happiness.'

It is a shame the media, not just in Egypt, have exaggerated reports of Salah's good work: millions and millions of Egyptian pounds to build schools, refurbish hospitals and mosques, to donate a dialysis machine and an ambulance, to help young couples get married, to be injected into the development fund founded by President el-Sisi. Much of it is true, but not all of it, such as the 8 million Egyptian pounds Salah is said to have allocated to buy and donate a five-acre plot for the building of a water purification plant. 'Fake news,' explains el-Bahnasy. 'It created false hope and disillusionment for many.'

The owner of the small bookshop has nothing further to add. But many in the village are quick to recall that people came from the neighbouring regions in search of charity, an endless pilgrimage in search of help that does not come from the government. 'The Salah family were confined to their house and if Mo had been a bank he would have gone bankrupt,' the mayor points out, sarcastically. The motivations and importance of Salah's charitable foundation now become clear.

Dark, wrinkled sods, grass scattered with ducks and hens, a long wall, a metal gate and a full-size football pitch: dirt, with a few sparse green patches. Almost an amphitheatre between red-brick houses and the minaret of the nearby mosque. This is the playing field of the Nagrig youth club, rechristened in tribute to Mohamed Salah after Egypt's qualification for the 2018 World Cup. A boy rides across the pitch on a bike while a small group are kicking a ball around barefoot. The youngest boys and girls are the most curious.

They come over to the new arrivals to ask for a photo in front of the centre's mural of a smiling Mo. It is impressive and brightly coloured, even if the hands giving a 'shaka' sign are not all that convincing. But it matters little. They are already lined up, posing for the camera, when a boy in full Liverpool strip stops playing to be snapped underneath the image of the man he wants to be. When he grows up.

Chapter 3
The first signature

A screaming mass of blue and yellow. Moving on and off a small dirt pitch through a gap in the metal fence. It sways from side to side, bringing up a cloud of dust in its wake. The kids from the Basyoun sports club will not stand still, not even for a moment. They group together, push and shove to make space to get a spot in the front row, to be seen and to peer at the foreigners who have just arrived.

When the name Salah is mentioned, all hell breaks loose. A chorus of 'Mohamed Salah! Mohamed Salah!' begins immediately. With the same strength, same intensity and same passion, albeit with fewer baritones, than in the Kop at Anfield. Still singing, the mass crosses the dual carriageway without paying attention to the cars, lorries and carts. The budding footballers accompany the visitors as they make their first stop on Salah's long journey: Ittihad Basyoun. In truth, there is little to see: the club building and two pitches, one seven-a-side and the other full-size, in a pitiful state. It's impossible to play here. Renovations are said to be on the cards, including the stands. When? No one knows. The blue and yellow shirts are joined by every imaginable colour, growing in number as the minutes pass. They form a swarm around the newcomers. There are so many kids in these parts. Something not seen in Europe, where birth rates are falling and populations are ageing. The opposite is happening in Egypt: the country has been experiencing a

demographic boom for decades; the population is approach-
ing 105 million and could reach 150 million by 2050. More
than a third of Egyptians are aged under fifteen. Two thirds
under 30. It is a very young nation and a ticking social time
bomb, given that economic growth is failing to rise hand in
hand with demographic growth. El-Sisi's government has
described the problem of overpopulation as one of the greatest threats facing Egypt, on a par with Islamism and terrorism. It has been trying, somewhat timidly, to tackle it with a
two-child policy aimed at limiting population growth among
the poorest families.

But there are no numbers here on the pitch at Ittihad
Basyoun, just smiling faces with dark hair and dark eyes.
There is Mohamed Eihofy, Mustafa Helmy Eid, Ahmed Sayeyu
and Mohamed Mansur: they are all aged between twelve and
thirteen. No one speaks anything other than Arabic. Only
the odd word of English learned at school. But it doesn't matter ... football is universal. Messi, Ronaldo, Neymar, Mbappé,
Real Madrid, Barcelona, Roma, Manchester United, City and
Liverpool are all names they know, if pronounced slightly
oddly, but everyone understands. With the help of an interpreter, they all want to have their say, in unison. Some shout
that Mo is the greatest, others that they play on the right
wing as well and others still that they're certain they are
left-footed too and can impress with their dribbling. Some
swear they are going to score lots of goals and want to go to
England to play one day, like Mo. Some ask what team you
support or take the ball to demonstrate what they can do,
right there and then. Others ask the visitors for a kick about,
while some simply explain how to get to the industrial insti-
tute where Mo studied, the school that General Ahmed Daif
Saqr, the region's governor, has decided to rename after its
most famous student. Their coach comes over to insist on

quiet and that they raise their hand, one by one, to speak. The kids do as they are told … up to a point. They listen when he tells a story they have probably heard a hundred times already: 'When he was twelve, Mohamed Salah played here in Basyoun, at this club, on this pitch. Sometimes his father would bring him; sometimes he would come on his own. He would come by minibus from Nagrig, about ten kilometres away. He only played here for one season, if I remember correctly, from 2004–05. Then, because he was so good, he went to Osmanson Tanta.'

Tanta, halfway between Cairo and Alexandria, is the capital of the Gharbia Governorate, which, with half a million inhabitants, is the fifth most populous area in the country. It boasts an important cotton industry and is famous, according to tourist guides, for its sweets and festivals held in honour of the Islamic Sufi Ahmad el-Badawi, founder of the Badawiyyah confraternity in the 13th century. His remains are buried in the city's main mosque. Tanta was the target of Isis terrorism on 9 April 2017, Palm Sunday. A suicide bomber blew himself up during mass in the Coptic church of Saint George. Twenty-eight people were killed and dozens wounded. The attack was followed shortly afterwards by another bomb in Saint Mark's Cathedral in Alexandria, this time killing seventeen. President Abdel Fattah el-Sisi declared a state of emergency, extended on several occasions, after the attack of 24 November 2017 on a mosque near El-Arish in the north of Sinai: 305 victims, including 27 children. The state of emergency – which allows the government to put civilians on trial in state security courts, intercept and monitor all forms of communication, impose censorship before publication, declare a curfew and place limits on public gatherings and media freedom – is still in force today. And it can be felt. Especially in Cairo, in the constant checks, the military presence, the watchtowers manned by armed soldiers, the concrete barriers protecting public buildings and embassies, and the metal detectors at hotel entrances.

But here, right in the heart of Tanta, amid the hustle-and-bustle of the market and the station, the state of emergency is not apparent.

The offices of the Egyptian Football Federation are on the fifth floor of a shabby building, above two busy cafés with tables looking out at the chaotic traffic. Regional cups and trophies are on display beyond a glass door. Mojtar el-Ashual is reading the sports pages of the newspaper quietly behind a desk. 'Of course Mohamed Salah played here, I remember it. Back then he was a boy, about so tall,' Mojtar makes a gesture with his hand. 'Now he's the pride of the Egyptian people. For me, he's as good as Messi and Ronaldo. One of the three best footballers in the world.' After chatting, he provides some useful tips. The federation official writes down two addresses where 'they can give you specific information about Salah.'

The second stop on the trail of Salah is the Tanta SC stadium. The team was founded in 1920, making it one of the oldest in the country. Tanta play in Egypt's second division and are known as the Sons of el-Badawi.

Refuge from the merciless sun can be found in the belly of the stadium, where Khaled Yousef el-Sharkawy, the director of the sports complex, does the honours. It is just a few steps up to the ring of oval seats, built in the 1920s, surrounded by tall skyscrapers. The capacity is for 20,000 fans, although one of the ends is currently undergoing renovations. A few yards away from the renovation work, an iron door leads to a patch of dirt. El-Sharkawy explains: 'It was once the training ground, where Salah trained. We want to fix it up and erect a statue right here in his honour.'

The tour continues past two swimming pools – one Olympic-sized, the other with a ten-metre springboard – to the headquarters of the Ministry of Youth and Sports for the Gharbia Governorate. Mohamed Ismail, the undersecretary, is busy in a heated meeting. But he finds five minutes to talk about the Salah phenomenon. He says he is an example not just for young people in Egypt but for the Arab world as a whole. He claims he has 'won people's hearts with his simplicity and humility, for being a good person who embodies the values of Islam. Something much more important than being a good footballer. He has managed to make himself loved in England, which certainly cannot be easy. And, of course, the pose he does when he scores, praying in front of a whole stadium. It helps break down cultural prejudices at a time when Islamophobia is on the rise in Europe.' An image that some have said seems to have been created deliberately to export a smiling and positive image of Egypt, to overshadow the economic crisis, the government, the repression and so on? The undersecretary does not take kindly to the suggestion; he replies that 'Greece and Portugal have also experienced extremely hard economic situations. Egypt is not the only country to have gone through a difficult period, but we're working to get out of it.'

The third stop is a large red building by the motorway to Alexandria. Access to the eighth floor is granted only after documents are checked. Tarek Omara, with a long face and delicate moustache, warmly welcomes the visitors into his office. The director of public relations at Osmanson Tanta suggests a Turkish coffee or tea before disappearing for five minutes on finding out Salah is the subject of the day. He returns with two photocopied sheets. One is a standard form with sections to be filled out. A black and white chequered ball stands out in the middle of the first page, with the logo of the Egyptian federation to the left. The photo ID of a boy with very short hair and a piercing gaze is attached to it with a paper clip. The poor quality of the photocopy is clear to see. Arabic script flutters underneath. It reads:

Player registration and agreement document

Season: 2005/06
Category: U14
Name: Mohamed Salah Hamed Ghali
Identity document: 160338 issued on 6/2002
Nationality: Egyptian
Date of birth: 15/6/1992
Place of birth: Nagrig, Basyoun
Province: Gharbia
Residence: Nagrig
School certificate: primary school
Current profession: student

I, the undersigned, Mohamed Salah Hamed Ghali, whose details are shown above, consent to joining the club: Osmanson Tanta.

I, the undersigned: Salah Hamed Mehrez Zaki Ghali, guardian of Mohamed Salah Hamed Ghali, give my consent for him to be enrolled at the Osmanson Tanta club.

The Osmanson Tanta club gives its agreement to enrol the player Mohamed Salah Hamed Ghali in the Under 14 squad for the 2005–06 season.

The club has completed the player's medical assessment and verified his ability to play the sport of football under its responsibility. The club also recognises its obligation to pay all the financial rights of the player in keeping with the regulations.

The club's stamp and three signatures appear at the bottom: Mo Salah, Salah Hamed Mehrez Zaki Ghali, his father and guardian, and the club representative.

It is the first contract, the first important signature in Mohamed Salah's life. A thirteen-year-old boy, one metre 69 centimetres tall, weighing 68 kilograms, according to the second page of the photocopy, which also shows the list of the names of ten players sent to the football federation to formalise their registration and transfer. Mo is in eighth position, preceded by another boy from Nagrig: Abdel Amid Ragab, born in the same year.

The Osmanson PR director explains that the club was founded a few months before the start of the 2005–06 season, when it began recruiting boys for the Under 14s.

Osmanson Tanta is a football club directly descended from the Arab Contractors Sporting Club, also known as El Mokawloon, the Cairo club. To be clear, Arab Contractors is one of the largest engineering and construction firms in Egypt and the Middle East. Founded in 1955 by Osman Ahmed Osman – a businessman and politician, as well as Minister of Housing and Development under Sadat's presidency – the company was involved in the construction of major public works, such as the Aswan Dam, Luxor and Sharm el Sheikh airports, the Bibliotheca Alessandrina and the Desert Road. In 1973, Arab Contractors founded its football club that plays in the Egyptian Premier League and boasts three African Cup Winners' Cups (1982, 1983 and

1996) a league title (1983), three Egypt cups (1990, 1995 and 2004) and a Super Cup (2004). In the early 21st century, under the presidency of Ibrahim Mahlab, who would be prime minister between 2014 and 2015, it launched a campaign to discover new talent and created satellite clubs, such as Osmanson Tanta, to receive and nurture promising young players. But how did Mo Salah come to arrive at this outpost of Arab Contractors? Tarek Omara denies that the boy was selected thanks to the Pepsi League, at the tournament played with his school in Nagrig. The scout theory, the Reda theory, comes back up but is unconfirmed. What is certain is that Salah only played one season at Osmanson, from 2005 to 2006. The coaches immediately realised how good the boy was and sent him to Cairo. It was this that led to the inclusion of a line in the 2007 El Mokawloon annual report, under the heading of 'Other News': 'The club has signed an attacking midfielder: Mohamed Salah.'

Chapter 4

The long journey

Two men, wearing grey shirts and black trousers, are sitting under a large white umbrella. Auad Nagui el-Hoshy and Ali Abdel Tawab are there to supervise one of the entrances to the enormous Arab Contractors Sporting Club in Nasr City. It is a twenty-minute journey, traffic permitting, from Tahrir Square: the 6th October Bridge offers views down over Ramses Square, the beating heart of the megalopolis, and the Abbassia district, with Saint Mark's Coptic Cathedral, the minarets of the Al-Rahman Al-Rahim mosque and the City of the Dead, the huge Islamic cemetery of Al-Qarafa that is home to more than half a million graves. Here, among the skyscrapers under construction and the Arab Contractors Medical Centre, is El Mokawloon's stadium.

Auad and Ali welcome the visitors warmly, proffering two plastic chairs. They explain that a permit is required to tour the club's sports facilities. Only club members can go beyond the barrier. So, between a phone call and a fax, waiting for authorisation, as well as one car going in and another coming out, the topic of conversation is Mohamed Salah. His latest matches, his latest goals, Liverpool, Real Madrid, PSG, Barcelona and the Egyptian national side. The two gatekeepers know plenty about the Pharaohs' number 10. They pull out their phones to proudly show off selfies taken with him the last time he visited. They explain that Mo is a humble person, friendly and kind, someone who does not put on airs

and graces. They remember when he was just a kid from his
village in the Nile Delta and the time he once had to sleep
in the night watchman's hut.

Mohamed Salah has been on a very long journey indeed.
A two-kilometre walk or bike ride across the jasmine and
onion fields from Nagrig to Ash Shin. From there a minibus
to Basyoun. From Basyoun to Tanta, from Tanta to Cairo's
Ramses Square, then another minibus to El Mokawloon.
During rush hour, passengers are always packed into the
minibuses like sardines. So much so that, as Mohamed Abo
Hatab, a childhood friend and teammate of Salah, remembers: 'Sometimes I had to help Mo in through the window
to get a seat for both of us.' Four to four-and-a-half hours
there, four to four and a half hours back, five days a week.
The fourteen year old from Nagrig's alarm clock would go
off at 7am for school, from 8am to 9.30am. Then it was off to
Cairo. Arab Contractors had provided him with an exemp-
tion, a letter allowing the boy to miss class so he could get to
the pitch by 2.30pm. Training began at 3.30pm and finished
at 6pm. He would have a quick shower, then run to catch
the four or five minibuses home. If all went well, he would
arrive between 10 and 10.30pm. There was just time to have
dinner and go to bed. The same routine would start all over
again the next day. It was a tough, very tough life for a fourteen year old. But as he would say years later: 'You don't get
anything without giving something. And I've always been
capable of making lots of sacrifices for football.'

Sacrifices his mother did not understand. She worried
about all the hours of travelling. She was afraid something
would happen to him and would have preferred him to be
at home with his brothers and sisters. And to make things
worse, whenever she called his mobile to make sure everything was OK, Mo hardly ever answered. He would snore

his way through the minibus journey back to Nagrig. In that deep, unwakeable sleep of teenage boys. But mothers will always worry. Salah Hamed Mehrez Zaki Ghali, Mo's father, himself a former footballer, would calm her down by saying: 'Let him play. Later on, we'll see.'

The best solution, as the boy loved football so much, was the thing he liked the most. And he had no intention of stopping. He dreamt, like millions of his peers, of becoming a professional footballer, of being on TV, of being recognised in the street. Perhaps even of winning the title of best African footballer one day. It was already a lot to hope for. He did not dare think about anything bigger than that. Who were his idols? Zinedine Zidane, for his magic, his Marseille turns and his class; Ronaldo, the Brazilian phenomenon who scored two goals against Germany at the 2002 World Cup Final in Japan and South Korea; and Francesco Totti, the Roma captain, for his loyalty to the Giallorossi shirt, for his vision of the game and the power and guile of his left-footed shots. Then, of course, there was the home-grown idol: Mohamed Aboutrika.

A cigarette, a sip of boiling hot tea and the time chatting with the two watchmen flies by. They do everything they can to put their guests at ease and assist them with the challenging task of getting the green light. But the authorisation does not come. Like elsewhere, bureaucracy in Egypt is no joke. Luckily, Captain Hamdy Nouh, the man Mo Salah considers a second father, or rather, his spiritual father, arrives right on time for his appointment. Tall, skinny, with a thin face, grey hair and a grey moustache, his voice hoarse from so many cigarettes, Hamdy Nouh greets Auad and Ali warmly and loads the visitors into his car. The bar is finally raised. Once past the gatekeepers, the tour of the Arab Contractors' sports facilities can begin. Starting with the 35,000-seater

Osman Ahmad Osman Stadium, the seven artificial and grass training pitches, tennis courts, basketball and volley-ball courts, Olympic-sized pool, hotels, a restaurant overlook-ing the hill, bars and cafés, and the club players' residence. There is even a petting zoo to keep the youngest fans happy. Captain Hamdy parks up and walks towards his office, right next to the pool, where a dozen kids are happily splashing about while their mothers, wearing head scarves, sit at the tables of the outdoor café. The office contains a desk, a TV, a computer and plenty of papers and books. On the wall hangs a large photo of a younger Hamdy Nouh, with a head full of dark curls and wearing the yellow and black striped shirt of El Mokawloon. Mohamed Salah's second father is now 63 and gladly talks about his past and how lucky he was to coach Mo.

'I was a striker, a number 10. I started playing for Esco when I was seventeen. I stayed there for seven seasons before I was sold to Arab Contractors in exchange for the construction of a medical centre and a textile company. I scored 77 goals here and wore the national team shirt at the 1980 African Cup of Nations. I saw out my playing career at Ismaily and started coaching when I was 34. Always kids: Under 13s, Under 15s and Under 17s. First in the United Arab Emirates, then, from 2004, after specialising in France, at Clairefontaine, I came back to this club.'

It was during the 2006–07 season that he met the boy from Nagrig.

The decision to bring Salah from Tanta to Cairo had not been his. It was down to another former glory of Egyptian football: Captain Riou, the playing name of Refaat Ragab, a fast winger who was part of the Ismaily team that won the African Cup of Champions Clubs in the Cairo stadium in front of 130,000 fans on 9 January 1970. 'Salah was small and thin, but determined and intelligent. Some of his qualities were God-given,' Captain Riou would remember some time later. 'Others were down to the training he'd been given. He deserved an opportunity.'

'The first time I saw him I realised he had talent. He was left-footed, very quick and although he was only fourteen he already had a professional way of looking at the game,' explains Captain Nouh. What was the boy like? 'Shy, polite, he didn't talk much but would smile from ear to ear and listen carefully to the advice I gave him. His response was always the same: "OK Coach, thanks Coach." I also remember him complaining. When he started growing at fifteen, his knees ached and I decided not to let him play. Tears streamed down his cheeks. Or when we were 0–1 down after the first half and I found him sobbing in the corner. He came on in the second half and scored two goals. Mohamed was very competitive, he hated not being able to play or losing a match.'

Captain Nouh goes over to his desk and takes a photo out of a packet of papers. The full El Mokawloon youth team line up. The coach, wearing a yellow and black shirt and the number 20 on his chest, stands on the far left. Crouching, a little further on, with short hair and a grimace on his face, is a very young Momo. What were you able to teach him? 'I worked with him on his psychology, football and technique. If you want to become a great player, if you want to make your family and your country happy, I told him, you have to train and train and get better as a player and as a person. In terms of football, I tried to pass on my experience as a player, the meaning and responsibilities of being a professional. Technically, I insisted over and over again that he had to use his right foot as well as his left. I would tell him and keep repeating it. And I remember when the club management decided to have Mo live here in the residence, we would meet at 6am, after prayers, on the training ground, to work on the little details, to refine his qualities and get the best out of his right foot.'

Captain Nouh coached Salah for two seasons but has never lost touch with him. Now, whenever they meet up or he sees him on television he is delighted. 'I'm so happy to see how far he's come. I wasn't convinced of it. When his father would call me to ask how things were going with Mohamed, I would say: "Your son is going to go a long way, a very long way." But if I'm honest, I didn't expect he would be able to do what he's done with Liverpool. He deserves it. He deserves everything God's given him because he's a good person, religious and generous.'

Said el-Shishini takes up the baton from Captain Nouh. He coached Salah at Under 16 and Under 17 level at El Mokawloon. He is keen to share his memories with the guests: 'When I met him he was playing as a left-back. I had four boys in the same position: Ali Fathi, Abo Hatab, Sherif Alaa and Younes. There wasn't much chance of Salah making the starting eleven. He was the third choice. Partly because the long journey back and forth from Nagrig was tiring him out, physically and mentally. Mohamed Elneny had the same problem. I spoke to Ibrahim Mahlab, the president, and explained that I had two promising players from the youth sector that were wasting time and focus by travelling back and forth to Cairo. Mahlab decided to offer them the chance to stay in the club's residence. It was a gesture that allowed them both to make a difference.'

The coach stops, thinks for a moment and then continues talking about what, as far as he was concerned, was the turning point for Salah.

'I remember we had an away game with the Under 16s

in the Cairo Youth League. It was a difficult match against a tough rival, ENPPI [a team owned by an Egyptian oil and gas company]. We won 4–0. It was a fantastic result! We were all celebrating, except Mohamed, who was crying in a corner of the dressing room because he hadn't scored. He'd tried at least five times. Coming out of defence, he had made it to a one-on-one with their keeper, but, shattered from his run, he missed. His teammate, Zika, scored a hat-trick. I took the two boys to one side. I gave Zika 50 pounds as a reward and gave 25 to Salah, even though he hadn't scored. And I promised him he would have other chances to score and that, one day, he would become the team's top scorer. I didn't just say it for the sake of it, I understood from his anger, from his tears, just how passionate he was about scoring goals. And during training, I realised he had the characteristics and speed to stay up front. I tried moving some of the players around, put Ali Fathi at left-back and Mohamed on the right wing. It worked beautifully. Salah played in the Cairo Youth League with the U16s and in the Nationwide League with the U17s. He ended up scoring 35 goals.'

Salah's long journey had a happy ending. At aged sixteen, he was called up to the first team by Mohamed Radwan. According to Radwan, the former coach of the Under 14s, Mohamed Abdelaziz, nicknamed Zizo, took a personal inter-est in the young right-winger. He gave him targeted training to get the best out of his pace, to make sure he did not hold onto the ball too much, a problem he was having at that time, and could widen his vision of the game. Mohamed made a real effort. The results were clear to see and his coaches were satisfied. 'He is a boy who focuses on what he's doing, comes to training on time and works hard to improve his weaknesses.' His teammates saw him as a 'hadi', a quiet, modest guy who got on with his job and, in the evening, after a dinner of soup, grilled chicken and green salad, would go up to bed in room number 510 of the residence overlooking the training grounds. Unlike many of his peers at the residence, he did not like staying up late. He joked with his teammates but was not a fan of classic dressing room pranks. He enjoyed playing with the PlayStation and at ping pong.

'I was living with footballers who had much more experience than me and looked after me. I was sixteen years old and I was in seventh heaven,' Mo Salah would say some time afterwards. If his dream was to become a professional footballer, it was about to become a reality. In the 2008–09 season, the boy from Nagrig played 23 minutes with the first team. He was as happy as happy could be.

It's getting late. Captain Nouh offers the visitors a lift. Down from the Arab Contractors hill, a taxi draws up alongside the City of the Dead. Battered, noisy, apparently lacking any shock absorbers, it is decorated like a Christmas tree with Salah photos, stickers and figurines, lit up in coloured lights in his honour. Captain Nouh was right: 'Mo is a phenomenon: he's won over an entire city and an entire country.'

Chapter 5

A year of great change

It was 6pm on 25 December 2010, the fourteenth matchday of the Egyptian Premier League season. Arab Contractors were playing away at Al Ahly. It was a tough match for El Mokawloon, given that they were languishing second from bottom in the table while the Red Devils were up in third. In the 56th minute, Arab Contractors fired the ball up from midfield. Mohamed Salah ran like lightning, leaving two red-shirted defenders in his wake. He controlled the ball, stood firm as one of the defenders came back at him, unleashed a left-footed shot on the diagonal and wrong-footed the keeper. Mo, wearing the number 31 on his back, brought his forefinger to the tip of his nose before kneeling on the turf to thank Allah and being swallowed up by his teammates in a group hug. It was his first league goal. His second in a yellow-and-black striped shirt after the one he had scored sixteen days earlier against Suez in the Egypt Cup.

One year on: 3.45pm on 26 December 2011, at the New Suez Stadium. The tenth game of the season. El Mokawloon, currently propping up the table, were playing Petrojet. Following a one-two just beyond the halfway line, Mohamed Salah picked up the ball in the area between three defenders in blue shirts. He proved quickest and toe-poked it past the opposing keeper and into the back of the net. It was his third goal of the 2011–12 season.

In the period between 25 December 2010 and

26 December 2011, profound changes had taken place in the Arab world, in Egypt and for Mo.

It all began in Tunisia. On 17 December 2010, Mohamed Bouazizi, a street vendor, set himself on fire to protest against ongoing police harassment in the town of Sidi Bouzid. His actions sparked protests across the country against the authoritarian regime of Zine El Abidine Ben Ali, who had been in power since 1987. It was a revolution against despotism, corruption, unemployment and the rising cost of food, as well as a demand for the democratisation of the policing system and better living conditions. A popular uprising with hundreds of deaths that led, in less than a month, to the collapse of the regime. On 14 January 2011, Ben Ali fled to Jeddah in Saudi Arabia.

Eleven days later, the spark of the Arab Spring caught light in Egypt. On 25 January, National Police Day, thousands of demonstrators were summoned over the Internet to descend on Cairo's streets. They were protesting against hunger, unemployment, the corrupt regime, sham elections some months earlier, and torture inflicted by the police. They shouted for 'bread, freedom and social justice.' They demanded democracy and the resignation of President Hosni Mubarak, who had been in power for 30 years. They were young people, non-politicised men and women, people from all social conditions: from the middle class to labourers and farmers. The uprising spread to other cities: from Alexandria to Tanta, from Mansura to Aswan. Clashes between the police and protesters intensified. The first deaths were reported and hundreds were arrested. Eighteen days of fury, blood, fire and great hope would follow. Eighteen days in which Tahrir Square became the centre of the world and the symbol of the Egyptian uprising. Days such as 28 January, the 'Friday of Anger', when dozens of people lost their lives in the streets of Cairo (by the end of the uprising there would be 846 dead and over 6,000 injured) as tanks and the army patrolled the streets. Days such as 2 February, when supporters of Mubarak stormed Tahrir Square, riding horses and camels to attack those who opposed the regime. But the protesters fought back. By now, the days of the regime were numbered. On 11 February 2011, President Hosni Mubarak left the position he had held since 1981 and fled to Sharm el Sheikh. The vice president Omar Suleiman announced that the Egyptian premier was leaving power in the hands of the Supreme Council of the Armed Forces. A night of nationwide celebration followed, with tears, hugs, kisses, singing and dancing. Red, white and black flags were waved across the country. With cries of 'Horreja! Horreja!' (Freedom!), without distinctions of class, sex, religion or political position, the Egyptian people celebrated liberation from the regime. The revolution had won, but the hopes of the Arab Spring would be short-lived. The spring had also turned football on its head. The Egyptian Premier League had been at a standstill since 27 January. It would resume, behind closed doors, on 13 April. The Egypt Cup was cancelled. The African Youth Championship, due to be held in Libya from 18 March to 1 April, was postponed due to the civil war that had broken out between forces loyal to Colonel Muammar Gaddafi and the rebels. The CAF subsequently decided to award the tournament to South Africa, where it was played from 17 April to 1 May.

Diaa el-Sayed, the Egyptian Under 20 coach, called up players who had impressed in the first half of the league season for the continental tournament. Players like Ahmed el-Shenawy, the Al-Masry keeper, Omar Gaber and Mohamed Ibrahim from Zamalek. Mohamed Salah, who had posted a number of good performances and scored some important goals, was no exception. The young Pharaohs were drawn in Group A and would face Lesotho, Mali and South Africa. The top two teams in each group would qualify for the FIFA U20 World Cup, to be held in Colombia in July. Egypt's first Under 20 game was played against Lesotho in Johannesburg on 17 April. They won easily, 2–0. The scoring was opened by Ahmed Hegazi – the Ismaily central defender – with a peremptory header. The result was sealed by number 12 Mohamed Salah with a confident penalty in the 64th minute. It was his first goal in a red Pharaohs shirt. The second game had a nasty surprise in store. Ten-man Mali held their ground against el-Sayed's boys and Amara Konate beat Ahmed el-Shenawy from the penalty spot. The Pharaohs would face the hosts in their final U20 game. A draw against South Africa would have been enough to take them to the World Cup in Colombia but the match ended in a 1–0 win thanks to a goal from Mohamed Hamdy. Egypt were into the tournament's semi-finals and had clinched their ticket to South America! Everyone was celebrating except Salah. 'After the game he went into his room, closed the door and started crying,' Diaa el-Sayed would remember some time later. 'He didn't even want to come to dinner. I asked him why. He said he had missed too many scoring chances. It was true. In the second half, he must have missed at least fifteen. We won anyway, but the boy couldn't rest so the next day we went to the training ground. It was me, him and the ball. I spent a whole hour feeding him the ball from various positions so he could practise shooting and scoring. The rest of the team turned up and began cheering him on. When we finished, I took him to one side and said: "Now you'll see how good you can be in front of a goal."'

Mohamed Salah failed to score in the semi-final against Cameroon on 28 April. Egypt lost on penalties (4–2), but the Pharaohs did not leave the tournament empty-handed. On 1 May, they beat Mali 1–0 in the third place play-off to win the bronze medal. Diaa el-Sayed was satisfied with third place. And he was happy with how much promise the young Pharaohs had shown: Ahmed el-Shenawy, who had conceded only a single goal from open play in five matches, won the Best Goalkeeper award. All the others had played well too.

What about Mo? He had made an excellent impression, even if he did lack sharpness in front of goal. But the advice of his manager proved useful as he went on to score three goals for El Mokawloon in the league. One on 2 May against Petrojet and two in one game (for the first time ever) against Smouha on 26 May. The goals were very similar: he put on a burst of pace, like a motorbike at full throttle, leaving opponents in his wake before striking the ball confidently with his left foot. Great goals, there was no doubt about it. Goals and performances that earned him the interest of a number of clubs in Egypt and beyond. This was nothing new. 'At the start of his career, an agent offered Salah the opportunity to go to Germany,' remembers Mohamed Amer, the former Arab Contractors coach. 'But without the right club visa. He thought about it seriously because, like a lot of players, he dreamt of playing in Europe. When I found out, I spoke to him and advised him not to take any rash decisions that might damage his career.' The boy from Nagrig listened to his manager and the club offered him a new contract for 40,000 Egyptian pounds; Osama el-Saiedi, the Contractors Football Supervisor, publicly stated in October 2010 that Mohamed Salah, Mohamed Elneny and Ali Fathy were not for sale because they represented the future of the team. And to make things even clearer, he added: 'I hope agents will stay away from them because we are not ready to discuss any offers from Egyptian or foreign clubs.' But towards the end of the 2010–11 season, the offers came flooding in and it was the young eighteen-year-old Salah himself who talked about them: 'I received several offers from Ahly, Zamalek, Ismaily and Masry, but I prefer to play for Ahly. Playing for Ahly means more brightness and more reputation, the club's stability also helps any player to shine. The club's management will examine the several offers after the end of the season.'

The then coach of Al Ahly, the Portuguese manager Manuel José Oliveira, later confirmed that his club had been the front runner: 'I called the club president, Hassan Hamdy, to sign Salah and his teammate Bassem Ali. A few days later he told me that everything had been agreed and only the signatures of the players were missing.' But the deal did not take place because the Egyptian Football Association decided not to relegate any teams that season: despite finishing bottom of the table, Arab Contractors, 27 points behind title winners Al Ahly, would remain in the Premier League. According to Oliveira, this led the Arab Contractors president to change his mind and decide not to sell Salah. The Zamalek option did not come into play either, because Mamdouh Abbas, the then president of Cairo's other big club, was apparently unconvinced:

'He needs lots of work. He's a bit selfish, even if he is a big player. I like Elneny more,' he is said to have told one of his staff. Six years later, the by then former president of Zamalek would find himself in the stands at Anfield, invited by Mo, to admire that 'selfish' player scoring a wonderful goal against Chelsea. But that was not all; there is another version of how both Zamalek and Al Ahly ended up doing without the services of Salah. Sherif Habib, the president of Arab Contractors at the time, allegedly rejected the offer from both Cairo clubs in order to sell the striker to a European club, thus obtaining a two-fold advantage that would see the club bring in a few extra pounds as well as promoting it on new markets at the same time.

The nineteen year old from Nagrig ended the 2010–11 season with twenty appearances, 1,256 minutes of playing time, four goals in the Egyptian Premier League and one in the cup. He knew he would be wearing a yellow-and-black striped shirt again next season. But first there was a World Cup to think about.

Barranquilla, 29 July 2011, the Estadio Metropolitano Roberto Meléndez, Egypt-Brazil, the first game in the FIFA U20 World Cup. The opening ceremony involved an array of colours, music, folklore and Colombian dancing. After the grand finale came to an end with fireworks, the referee blew his whistle to start the match. It took only eighteen seconds for Mohamed Salah to show what he could do. He stole the ball from Danilo and sped off down the right wing before cutting back into the middle and unleashing a shot that ended up in the side netting. Despite being outnumbered by those of the Canarinha, the Egyptian fans cheered. The number 12 imposed himself again shortly afterwards as he made a run into the box, but his shot failed to trouble the Brazilian number 1. In the twelfth minute, Philippe Coutinho put in a perfect cross from the corner flag to allow Danilo to open the scoring from a header. One-nil. But Egypt did not let their heads go down. In the 26th minute, Danilo made a bad error when he failed to clear a cross from Sobhi from the left; Omar Gaber controlled the ball in the box and got the better of Gabriel. The score line remained unchanged at the end of the 90 minutes. For the young Pharaohs, a draw against the South American champions and four-time U20 World Cup winners was a success. Salah and his teammates even received compliments from

Ney Franco, the Brazil manager, who said in his press conference: 'Players like Mohamed Ibrahim and Mohamed Salah will have a bright future.' Egypt kept up their level. The young Pharaohs beat Panama 1–0 and overwhelmed Austria 4–0, qualifying for the round of sixteen behind Brazil with seven points. On 9 August, they played Argentina in Medellín. The game ended 2–1 to the Albiceleste. It was decided by three penalties, the first and extremely contentious of which came in the 42nd minute. Carlos Luque went down in the area and the referee took the bait. Érik Lamela stepped up for the spot kick. Ahmed el-Shenawy guessed right and got a hand to it, but the ball rolled into the back of the net. History repeated itself in the second half. Luque and Lamela combined again; this time, the latter's penalty gave the Egyptian keeper no chance. It looked as if it was all over, but then Adrián Martínez brought down Saleh Gomaa in the 70th minute. Salah stepped up to take the penalty and the number 12 made no mistake. The goalkeeper went one way; the ball went the other. The game was still on. The young Pharaohs kept trying but Andrade and then Leonel Galeano both denied the Africans in stoppage time.

Egypt's Under 20s would not repeat the third place they had delivered ten years earlier in Argentina, but, on balance, the tournament that was eventually won by Oscar and Willian's Brazil had been a positive one. 'Although they didn't have a chance to prepare properly because of the situation back home and the fact that the season ended much later than planned, the lads played well,' said el-Sayed, who also asked the fans to support this generation because they offered hope to the country.

There was no doubt that the young Pharaohs had given a good account of themselves, Mohamed Salah in particular. So much so that there were plenty of transfer rumours about

foreign clubs being interested in the El Mokawloon striker
when he returned home. In the meantime, he could be satisfied with a call-up to the senior national team, although this
time this was actually the Under 23 Olympic team … the
explanation is a little complicated. Under Hassan Shehata,
known as 'El Me'alem' (The Boss), the Pharaohs had won
three consecutive Africa Cup of Nations (2006, 2008 and
2010) but qualification for the final stages of the 2012 tournament turned into a nightmare. Two defeats and two draws
left the Pharaohs languishing at the bottom of Group G, with
only two points from four games. On 6 June 2011, Hassan
Shehata tendered his resignation after a draw at home to
South Africa. Criticised for not bringing younger players
into the team, The Boss was eventually accused of displaying excessive religious fervour and providing unconditional
support to the Hosni Mubarak regime. This was a choice for
which the demonstrators in Tahrir Square could not forgive
him: 'You have insulted the youth that supported you in winning three cups. You sided with tyranny against freedom,'
read one of the comments on an *Ahramonline* article about
the manager.

The EFA did not appoint a successor to Shehata and
decided instead that the Under 23 Olympic side would
play the final two 2012 Africa Cup of Nations qualifying
games, under Hany Ramzy – a former defender for Al Ahly,
Neuchâtel Xamax, Werder Bremen and Kaiserslautern,
who had 124 international caps and years of managerial
experience behind him. The games against Sierra Leone
and Niger were an opportunity to help the boys mature and
prepare them in the best way possible for the final stage of
the Olympic Games qualifiers. Ramzy knew Mohamed Salah
well and rated him. He had selected him for the Olympic
side training camp and, in May, for the friendly against Chad

and two games against Sudan (4 and 18 June), qualifiers for the 2012 London Olympics. It was no surprise that Mo was called up to play Sierra Leone in Freetown on 3 September. Salah made his full international debut aged nineteen years, two months and nineteen days, although in reality he was lining up with the Under 23s. He was still on the pitch at the end of 90 minutes, but his debut was not what had been hoped for. The Leone Stars won 2–1. They sent the home fans at the National Stadium in Freetown into raptures and robbed the Pharaohs of their last chance to qualify for the 2012 Africa Cup of Nations. Consolation came in Cairo in the final qualifying game on 8 October. The Pharaohs swept Niger aside 3–0, with two goals from Marwan Mohsen and Salah's first in an Egypt shirt. In the 56th minute, Mo – wearing the red number 8 – and Mohamed Elneny pulled off a one-two in midfield. Salah got the ball back from his Arab Contractors teammate, who issued him with an invitation to beat the opponents' offside trap. Mo beat Mohsen to it and slotted an angled left-footed shot past the keeper. He smiled as he was hugged by his teammates and then pointed to the bench to celebrate with his manager. It was a shame the match was being played behind closed doors.

The following day, 9 October 2011, ended in a bloodbath following a Coptic Church protest. The Christian minority had taken to the streets of Cairo in protest against the governor of Aswan province who had set fire to a church a few days earlier. The demonstrators were attacked and dozens of people lay in the streets of the Egyptian capital. These were the most dramatic clashes since the Tahrir Square uprising. Although Egypt had seemed to be moving towards a democratic transition following the constitutional referendum in March and with elections on the horizon, it now appeared to be descending back into chaos. On 10 October, the EFA announced that it would not host the 2012 Olympics African qualifying tournament that was scheduled to take place from 26 November to 10 December. The beginning of the tournament coincided with parliamentary elections that would require maximum security. The league season did, however, resume as planned on 14 October. In the third game, away at Smouha, Salah scored his first goal of the 2011–12 season.

On 26 November 2011, the final qualifying stages for the London Olympics began in Morocco, chosen by CAF to replace Egypt. Hany Ramzy's Under 23s were drawn in Group B in Marrakesh and would face Gabon, Ivory Coast and South Africa. They played their first game on 27 November. Egypt 1-Gabon 0. They stuttered in their second match as Koné scored for Ivory Coast in the 82nd minute. In the third, they beat South Africa 3–0.

The young Pharaohs qualified for the semi-finals and would play the home side in Tangier on 7 December. Things did not go well … They were already two goals down by the ninth minute. Salah reduced the deficit in the 36th minute, firing the ball into the bottom right-hand corner from the edge of the area. But the game ended 3–2 to Morocco. It was time for another third place play-off, with the winners going straight to the London Olympics. The losers would face a play-off against an Asian opponent in April 2012. The young Pharaohs wasted no time and coolly dismissed Senegal 2–0. The U23s would play at the Olympics after a twenty-year absence!

By the end of 2011, Egypt's elections were in full swing. The results of the second round of voting to elect the 498 representatives of the People's Assembly (the Lower House) were revealed on 24 December. The Freedom and Justice Party, the political arm of the Muslim Brotherhood, had secured 36 per cent of the vote; the far-right Al-Nour Party had obtained 24 per cent, while the liberal democratic Wafd party had won 13 per cent. The third round of voting would be held on 11 January.

The end of 2011 brought further satisfaction to Mohamed Salah. On 31 December, he scored his fourth goal since the beginning of the season against El Gouna. That same day, *Al-Ahram*, the long-standing Middle Eastern publication, revealed its list of the top ten Egyptian footballers of the year. Strictly in alphabetical order: Abdallah Said, Ahmed Eid Abdel Malek, Ahmed Fathy, Ahmed Hassan, Ahmed Hegazi, Ahmed el-Shenawy, Hosni Abd Rabo, Hossam Ghaly, Mahmoud Abdel-Razek 'Shikabala' and, last but not least, Mohamed Salah. How did the boy from Nagrig manage to make the list? Because the Arab Contractors star 'is one of Egypt's hottest prospects. Salah exhibited impressive skills that left defenders trailing in his wake. The twenty-year-old player is fast, talented and is as efficient on both flanks as he is good using both legs. However his accuracy in front of goal has yet to improve.'

Chapter 6

Port Said

'I wanted to pay a tribute to the victims of the stadium in Port Said, where so many fans died because of tragic clashes. And to be clear, no one has ever asked me to put this number on the jersey. It's something I felt inside and chose to do it,' this was how Mohamed Salah explained to the *Liverpool Echo* in 2017 why he had chosen the number 74 shirt while he was at Fiorentina.

In 2018, he answered another question asked about the Port Said massacre by *L'Équipe Magazine*. 'It was a great sadness for Egypt. It was a very difficult thing to go through. For everyone. Still today it's hard for me to find the words to talk about it.'

'The biggest disaster in Egypt's football history,' as it was described at the time by Hesham Sheiha, the deputy health minister, decided the fate of men and women alike and changed the lives of many, including that of Mohamed Salah.

Mo's year had started with plenty of goals. On 5 January 2012, the twelfth matchday of the Egypt Premier League, he had scored the goal to make it 2–1 during a home game against Al-Ittihad. It was one of his usual dashes up the pitch that ended with his left foot. Four days later, he scored twice in the game that saw Arab Contractors take on El Dakhleya. Two goals in a 4–1 win. He had found the back of the net seven times in thirteen league games … not bad for a player criticised for his lack of sharpness in the box! No, Mohamed

Salah was no longer the boy from Nagrig who was not keen on his school work and thought only about football. The teenager started believing that football could become his job when he signed his first contract with Arab Contractors, when he was earning 200 Egyptian pounds a month. He was no longer the left-back number 3 who wanted to score at all costs and started crying whenever he couldn't. No longer the sixteen year old who was more emotional than he had ever been in his life when his manager had told him: 'You will be with the first team tomorrow.' Nor was he even the player Zamalek had rejected because he was not yet mature enough to play for one of the capital's big teams. Mohamed Salah, who ran like crazy and scored with his left foot, was now one of the most promising players in Egyptian football, one of the stars of El Mokawloon, a player that many would have liked to have at their own club. He had matured and changed, just like the rest of the country. On 21 January, the official results of the three rounds of parliamentary elections saw, as expected, a victory for the Freedom and Justice Party, who won 47 per cent of the vote and 235 seats in the lower house. Elections for the Upper House would take place over the coming weeks and the transition would end in June with the election of the first president chosen by the people after 30 years of dictatorship. But the path to democracy and the pacification of the country was long and paved with violence and blood.

On Wednesday 1 February 2012, in Port Said – a coastal town with 600,000 inhabitants, 200 kilometres from Cairo at the northern end of the Suez Canal – a match was taking place on the seventeenth day of the league season. Al-Masry, the home team, faced Al Ahly. The game was due to start at 4pm but kick-off was delayed by 30 minutes due to a pitch invasion by local fans. The score line was 0–1 at half-time.

Fábio Junior had given the Red Devils the lead in the eleventh minute and the Cairo team seemed to have the better of the home side. But then Moamen Zakaria scored twice, in the 72nd and 82nd minutes, to make the score 2–1, with Abdoulaye Cissé adding one more in the 92nd minute to make it 3–1 to Al-Masry. This third goal prompted a second pitch invasion in celebration, followed by another five minutes later, after the final whistle. Thousands of Al-Masry fans streamed onto the pitch and the manhunt began. They ran after the Al Ahly players and towards the area occupied by the 5,000 Red Devils fans, whom they attacked with stones, sticks, clubs, bottles, knives and flares and forced up towards the top tier of the stands. The police seemed unable to react or to separate the two sets of fans. Panic ensued inside the stadium.

Mohamed Aboutrika, the Al Ahly star who had sought refuge with his teammates in the dressing room, told the club's TV channel in a phone call: 'The security forces left us. They did not protect us. There is no movement, no ambulances. A fan died right in front of me in the dressing room. It's horrible, a day that will never be forgotten. This isn't football, it's war.'

Karim Zekri, the Al-Masry captain said: 'We'd left our changing rooms and gone to the Ahly players' changing rooms to make sure they were OK, and there, we saw the disaster. I found corpses on the floor and most of the deaths were from suffocation. People were squashed together and ended up dying that way. I went out of the changing rooms to help the Ahly fans get out, I kept taking as many out of the stadium as I could and returning. The strange thing is that there were no police in the stands or in the player's tunnel where I was taking them out from.' Ehab Ali, the Cairo club's team doctor, spoke of 'a war that had been planned.'

Clashes continued both inside and outside the stadium; the final death toll reached 74, with more than a thousand wounded. It had been the bloodiest day since the start of the uprising on 25 January 2011. As soon as the news arrived in Cairo, the match between Zamalek and Ismaily was suspended. The fans there reacted by setting fire to the stands. The Zamalek Ultras converged on the home of Al Ahly as a gesture of solidarity towards their eternal rivals. They began chanting slogans against the Interior Minister and the Supreme Council of the Armed Forces.

The following day, the Al Ahly Ahlawy Ultras and Zamalek's White Knight Ultras came together in a procession to protest in front of the parliament building. Clashes with the police went on for days, resulting in further deaths. The day after, the newly installed parliament began its extraordinary session with a minute's silence. The speaker of the assembly, Mohamed Saad el-Katatni, declared that the clashes were the 'work of the devil' and that Egypt's revolution was 'in danger'.

The next day, and even as early as the night of the tragedy itself, everyone started asking what had happened on the pitch in Port Said and who was responsible. The negligent police and military were accused of being accomplices to the massacre. They had allegedly done nothing to prevent or stop the violence. There were some reports that they had even encouraged the bloodthirsty Al-Masry fans. Others wondered if the tragedy was a punishment for the security forces and groups such as the Al Ahly Ultras, who had been in the front line in the street protests of the 2011 uprising and were opposed to the military junta. Many, including the Muslim Brotherhood, alleged the involvement of the former president Hosni Mubarak's men to avenge the Battle of the Camels in cooperation with the police. They said it was a planned war, a punishment carried out just a few days after the lifting of the state of emergency to demonstrate that there could be no order or security without the iron fist of the military. It was a tragedy that submerged Egypt in chaos in an extremely delicate period. It was not a battle between rival fans, between ultras, between uneducated and unemployed youths who had made violence and fighting their reason for living, but a political showdown.

Egyptian football went into shock. Mohamed Aboutrika, Emad Moteab and Mohamed Barakat, senior members of the Al Ahly team, announced their retirement from football. The Red Devils' Ultras claimed they would not set foot back in the stadium until justice had been done. The management of the Egyptian Football Federation was dissolved due to its links with the former regime. On 11 March, the Egyptian Premier League, at a standstill since that night in Port Said, was suspended indefinitely.

Chapter 7

A done deal

Preparations for the London 2012 Olympics were challenging after the tragedy in Port Said and the suspension of the league. But Hany Ramzy, the manager of Egypt's Olympic team, had still managed to organise a training camp in the United Arab Emirates and a handful of friendlies to help his team get back to full strength for the games in the British capital in August.

Another friendly was added to this schedule, in Switzerland, against the country's domestic champions FC Basel in March. Having missed the two previous games following a three-match call-up with the full national side – now managed by the American Bob Bradley – this trip to Europe was an opportunity for Mohamed Salah to get back on track. The Arab Contractors' striker had not disappointed alongside the country's best players. He had even scored his second goal in five games in a Pharaohs' shirt on 27 February against Kenya. The boy from Nagrig was in great shape and looking forward to meeting up with his friends in the Olympic team. Especially because the match in Switzerland had the potential to change the course of his life ...

'In August 2011, I was sent to follow the U20 World Cup in Colombia,' remembers Roberto Crausaz, the former Argentina defender who played in Switzerland with Lugano before joining the recruitment team at Basel about fifteen years ago. 'From the start of the competition, I was intrigued by the performance of Egypt, who held Brazil to a 1–1 draw. I went to watch them play their second game of the tournament against Panama in Barranquilla. That was when I discovered Mohamed Salah! I saw him play three times – twice in the group stage and once in the last sixteen game they lost against Argentina – and it was the same every time: whenever he put on a burst of pace, he would change the course of the match. As soon as he had the ball, you could feel something was about to happen.'

Roberto Crausaz quickly reported his findings to Basel's head of recruitment, Ruedi Zbinden. In a detailed report, he highlighted 'astonishing explosiveness in his runs and impressive technique with the ball at his feet.' He also noted an obvious weakness when it came to finishing: 'Salah lacked calm in front of goal and would lose his head during one-on-ones. But that didn't stop us wanting to recruit him. The real question was whether he would be able to adapt to life in Europe and the rigours of its football.'

The Basel scout was not the only one to fall under the spell of the young Egyptian striker's talent at the U20 World Cup. Several European clubs expressed their interest to Salah's representatives, the most persistent of which was Newcastle United. The Magpies even got an agreement from the player in late August 2011. 'Newcastle will soon make an official offer to sign me. I don't think Contractors will refuse to let me play in the English Premier League,' Mo Salah told an *Al-Ahram* journalist after the tournament in Colombia. 'It's a dream for any player to play in one of the strongest league competitions in the world. I want to play abroad; I think this would be my next step.' But Salah's dream of playing in the Premier League would have to wait. It was true that Newcastle's scouting team had been after him and noticed his potential. It was true that Alan Pardew, the Magpies' manager, would have been delighted to have had Mo in his team, but in the end the negotiations came to nothing and the reason why is far from clear. According to Egyptian sources, everything hung on the fact that Newcastle were not keen to pay £500,000 for the year-long loan. And so, Salah would stay in Egypt.

Despite ongoing interest from the Cairo clubs Al Ahly and Zamalek, Basel took the lead. 'After the U20 World Cup in Colombia, we put things on the back burner. Although we made contact with his representatives, it wasn't the right time for him to come,' said Roberto Crausaz. 'But during the winter transfer window, our sporting director Georg Heitz took matters into his own hands.'

According to the former director of the Swiss club, who left his position in June 2017, there was not a great deal that needed to be done. When Georg Heitz talks about what happened behind the scenes of the transfer in the offices of his company HWH, overlooking the historical centre of the city on the Rhine, he describes it more as a gift from on high: 'In January 2012, I had a call from a German agent, Sascha Empacher, offering me an Egyptian striker called Mohamed Salah. He was trying to get his player over to Europe and was doing the rounds of all the clubs, I think. When I heard the name it rang a bell and it turned out our recruitment team had targeted him a few months earlier. I watched a few videos then showed them to the president Bernhard Heusler and the manager Heiko Vogel. We quickly decided he might be the ideal replacement for Xherdan Shaqiri, who was due to be transferred to Bayern Munich the following season. The idea was to have Mohamed come for a trial period. We had no doubts about his potential as a footballer but we wanted to know a little bit more about his personality. That's when we came up with the idea of a friendly. After the tragedy in Port Said, the Egyptian Olympic team needed to find places to play games outside the country to prepare for London. So we organised a match with Basel and offered Mohamed Salah the chance to stay an extra week to train with us and learn about our structure.'

The die was cast. Mohamed Salah landed at Basel-Mulhouse-Freiburg airport on March 2012. The Arab Contractors star arrived a day before his teammates to begin discussions with the Swiss champions. The following day, in the small lounge in the reception of the Hotel Baslertor in Muttenz, he met with Georg Heitz and the manager Heiko Vogel. 'He hardly spoke any English,' remembers the former sporting director. 'Ibrahim Azab, one of Empacher's colleagues, acted as interpreter. We sensed he was looking forward to playing the friendly and to showing he had the ability to take over from Shaqiri.'

A spoken agreement already existed between Basel and Arab Contractors. Back in Egypt, no one had been in any doubt about the future destination of the Olympic team's star since about ten days earlier: on 2 March, Osama el-Saidi, one of the managers of the Cairo club, announced he had received a firm offer: 'We're going to look at it and make a decision quickly,' he said. Three days later, it was the turn of the manager Mohamed Abdel-Samie to reveal 'that [his] player will go to Switzerland for a medical. Another step in his career, which, I hope, will result in a transfer.' For his part, Mohamed Salah did not beat about the bush by revealing his career plans before leaving the country: 'Basel is the first step in building my career in Europe. I hope it will be a real springboard to joining one of the big clubs.'

But on 16 March 2012, when the match in the small Stadion Rankhof kicked off at 6.30pm, Mohamed Salah was on the bench. The Egyptian side went toe to toe with the Swiss team, somewhat changed since their 7–0 humiliation against Bayern Munich in the last sixteen of the Champions League three days earlier. The score was 1–1 when Mo Salah finally made his appearance at the start of the second half. In the small, open-air stand opposite the dressing room tunnel, a hundred or so Egyptian fans greeted his arrival by waving red, white and black flags stamped with the eagle of Saladin. In the VIP area, Georg Heitz was sitting alongside the president Bernhard Heusler when Egypt's number 22 got his first touch: it did not come to anything but Salah put on a burst of speed from his second touch that clearly posed a problem for the South Korean Park Joo-Ho. Heusler turned to his colleague and said, with a hint of irony: 'What was that? I've never seen a player that fast in my life!'

The Basel president was immediately interested ... and it did not take long for him to be completely won over: in the 56th minute, the Arab Contractors striker charged towards the far post to cut off a cross coming in from Fathy on the left. Park Joo-Ho was up against it once again and all Salah had to do was toepoke the ball over the line and into the bottom of the net. The young forward celebrated the goal by kneeling to kiss the bright green turf of the Rankhof pitch before ending up in the arms of his teammates. Imagine the amazement and joy in the VIP stand, where Bernhard Heusler was already rubbing his hands with glee at the prospect of the deal he was about to do! To banish any last minute doubts, Salah stepped up again in the 85th minute: this time, he took advantage of a long clearance from the goalkeeper Ahmed el-Shenawy and a tentative back header from Kováč before beating three Basel players and slotting an impeccable strike under the bar from six yards out. His second goal of the evening gave him confidence he had convinced the Swiss champions. Georg Heitz remembers: 'We went to see him at his hotel after the game, which the Egyptians won 4–3. As you can imagine, he was smiling from ear to ear. He knew his performance had impressed our directors. He stayed on for the extra week trial period. He performed quite timidly at training to start with, probably because he thought he'd already shown what he needed to convince us to take him. But he got better as the sessions went on and Heiko Vogel, the manager, was over the moon by the end. He wanted to have him in his team at all costs.'

The epilogue of the transfer saga played out in Cairo almost a month later. Discussions had intensified since the friendly: emails and faxes between the two clubs had become more and more frequent. There was plenty on the line as the directors at Arab Contractors were well aware of the talent and market value of their player, who had since scored another two goals for the national side against Uganda and Chad.

Finally, on Sunday 8 April 2012, Georg Heitz arrived in the Egyptian capital to finalise the deal: 'I thought everything had been decided but I realised at that first meeting that we would have to start from scratch.' It would take almost two days and more than seven hours of negotiations for the various parties to come to an agreement based on a €2.5 million transfer. 'It was a lot of money for us,' says Georg Heitz. 'We had never spent that much on a player. It was also a risk. We'd never had an Egyptian at the club before and very few had ever been successful in Europe.'

The FC Basel website officially confirmed the transfer at 2am on 10 April 2012. Mohamed Salah had signed for the Swiss club until 2016. His four-year contract would come into effect on 15 June, his twentieth birthday. In the photo accompanying the statement, the future Rotblau player is all smiles, with a thin beard and short hair, wearing a simple hooded brown sweatshirt over a white t-shirt. Snapped in the corner of an office, there was no need for any fancy clothing. Mo Salah kept his comments for the FCB website: 'I really appreciated the way the directors and players welcomed me when I came to Switzerland in March. They immediately accepted me and that made my decision easier. It's like a dream has come true. Now it's up to me to repay their trust in me and make Egyptians proud by becoming a star in Switzerland.'

Chapter 8
Picasso

The transfer announcement was met with a lukewarm response. In Basel, they prefer actions to promises. In the north-west of Switzerland, just a few miles from both France and Germany, people tend to keep their feet on the ground. Although the jewels in the crown of the old medieval quarter are its Notre-Dame cathedral and the red sandstone town hall, this city of 40 museums is in step with progress. Crossed by the Rhine, it is a haven for banks and companies working in the chemical industry. Basel is cosmopolitan and forward-thinking, as demonstrated by the Roche Tower; opened in 2015, the glass staircase structure of the tallest skyscraper in the country is strangely reminiscent of a pyramid.

When Mohamed Salah arrived during the 2012–13 season, the building was still under construction. A bit like his career. He still needed to build everything in Europe and would have to carve out a place for himself at Switzerland's top club. 'FCB had won almost everything there is to win domestically since the early 2000s and, thanks to the European Cup, had even become an institution in Switzerland,' remembers the former Argentine player, Nestor Subiat, a scout for the club on the Rhine for almost fifteen years. 'After qualifying for the group stage of the Champions League in 2003 and reaching the quarter-finals of the UEFA Cup in the 2005–06 season, the club had just completed an outstanding year in which it reached the last sixteen of the Champions

League for the first time and achieved a cup-league double. Inevitably, these performances had attracted the attention of foreign clubs, so much so that there was a certain amount of interest in their best players. At the end of the 2011–12 season, the midfielder Granit Xhaka was transferred to Borussia Mönchengladbach for €8.5 million and Xherdan Shaqiri was headed for Bayern Munich with a €10 million price tag.'

When it came to starting the defence of their titles, Basel clearly had Mohamed Salah in mind to occupy the right wing, left vacant by Shaqiri. The only problem was that the adjustment of the new recruit from Arab Contractors was proving tougher than expected. The timing was not exactly ideal when it came to putting the twenty-year-old striker in the right frame of mind for this new challenge. Between May and July 2012, Salah had to honour a number of national team call-ups and spend plenty of time on the road just as the Swiss league season was about to start: 'Even then, Mohamed was a bit the victim of his own success,' says an insider at the Swiss club. 'At the same time as he was trying to acclimatise to his new life, he was also having to respond to the invitations of the Egyptian Federation. So for three months, he had to juggle the Olympic Games with the U23s, the qualifiers for both the Africa Cup of Nations and the World Cup with the senior national side, and a pre-season training camp and friendly with Basel.'

It was a lot for just one man! But Mo Salah coped very well: for his club, he topped off pre-season training with a stunning goal in a friendly against the Romanians from Steaua Bucharest; with Egypt, he shone for the national team and scored four times with three assists in the World Cup and CAN qualifying knock-out games. Despite a scare following a shoulder injury in late June away to the Central African Republic, his marathon summer continued with the

London Olympics, this time with the U23 generation. On 26 July 2012 in Wales, he was kept on the bench for the first half of Egypt's opening game, as his teammates were outclassed by Neymar's Brazil. The half-time score was 3–0. But, as if by magic, as soon as he set foot on the pitch at Cardiff's Millennium Stadium, the Pharaohs woke up and the balance of power was reversed. The number 11 taunted the Brazilian defence and ridiculed his opponents on the right wing. Marcelo was sent tumbling on several occasions. In the 76th minute, the Real Madrid defender was powerless, as were Thiago Silva and Oscar, reduced to the role of spectators as the Egyptian prodigy strung together piece of skill after piece of skill; he controlled the ball with his left foot then followed up with a flawless strike that fired the ball into the back of Neto's goal. The Seleção may have eventually won 3–2, but for 45 minutes Salah was more than a match for the South American stars. In the following matches, his left foot was on target on two more occasions against New Zealand (1–1) and Belarus (3–0). Despite elimination at the hands of Japan (3–0) in the last sixteen on 4 August, he had unsurprisingly been one of the players of the Olympic tournament. Mo Salah could now devote himself to his new club.

'The fans were getting impatient,' says Patrick Sauteur, loyal to the Rotblau for more than 30 years and a long-time season ticket-holder at the St Jakob-Park. 'His transfer had caused a stir and his performances for the Egyptian national sides promised much upfront alongside the Swiss internationals Alex Frei, Marco Streller and Valentin Stocker. We were looking forward to seeing what the anointed successor to Shaqiri could do.' Only four days after his exit from the Olympic Games, Mohamed Salah had already played sixteen minutes in the third round of Champions League qualifying against the Norwegians of Molde (1–1). Although he did not have much time to impress, the new number 22 shone in the two following games: on 12 August, on his debut in the Swiss league, he was involved in all three goals against FC Thun, most importantly winning a penalty converted by Marco Streller. Six days later, back at the St Jakob-Park, he was even better in the 2–0 win over FC Lausanne-Sport, accompanying his second assist for Streller with his first official goal in a red and blue shirt: 'There was talk in the stands that the club had unearthed a real gem,' says Alex, a regular in the Muttenzerkurve, home to the most ardent fans at the St Jakob-Park. 'He was so incredibly quick that everyone started calling him Usain Bolt. But as the games went on, we started seeing it a bit differently when he began squandering chances in front of goal. He was capable of making an enormous difference, but he never seemed to be able to finish. He missed such easy chances that we were tearing our hair out. He really needed to make progress in that area.'

Despite the early doubts about his ability to impose himself at the defending champions, Mohamed Salah remained focused on his objectives. He had one advantage: he did not speak Swiss German and still had little English. This limited his interaction with the media and allowed him to quietly find his feet at his new club. At the end of August, he left the Hotel Baslertor in Muttenz and moved into an apartment, where he lived on his own pending the arrival of his fiancée Magi. He was quickly adopted by his teammates at the club. 'Despite what people might think, he's not really all that reserved. He's respectful but not shy at all. Despite his difficulties in English, he was open, laughing and joking a lot. He's a great guy. Everyone liked him and that definitely helped a lot,' confirms Germano Vailati, the goalkeeper, who arrived in Basel that same year.

The Egyptian striker also found a confidant at the club in

the form of steward Pascal Naef. It was he who nicknamed him 'Momo' from the very beginning; it was also he who helped him explore the city and adjust to his new life in Europe. Salah soon found his favourite spots in Basel: the Aladin restaurant in the city centre near Barfüsserplatz and another Lebanese canteen called Habibi in Binningen. 'He liked coming to us and felt comfortable here,' remembers a former waiter at the restaurant. 'Life is so different. Here everyone is at home by 6 in the evening but in Egypt everyone's still outside at 9 o'clock. It was a shock. He had to adjust to this new culture, to the food and to the weather as well.'

At the end of the summer, Mo Salah was going through a difficult time: as his team were deprived of a place in the Champions League group stages by the Romanians of Cluj, the Egyptian striker was struggling to get his left foot to do the talking. In September, he had to content himself with two goals, one in the domestic cup competition against the amateurs of FC Amriswil and another in the league against Lausanne-Sport. In October, he stayed under the radar during a period marked by a change of manager: Heiko Vogel was replaced by former club captain Murat Yakin. 'The change was good for Salah,' says a former staff member. 'Not that he got on badly with Vogel, on the contrary, but Yakin had another, perhaps warmer approach. He took him under his wing and did a lot of work with him after training.'

'That's not wrong,' confirms Murat Yakin. 'He would often stay behind after the others for sessions in front of goal. Although it was difficult to communicate with him, he was open to comments and always listened. We had to be patient and, even if he didn't like it much, incorporate him gradually. The click came after three or four months when he started speaking English. He became much more a part of the group and that was reflected on the pitch.'

Most often cast in the role of bit-part player behind the Swiss duo David Degen and Valentin Stocker, Mohamed Salah rediscovered his efficiency in November. In the Europa League, he made his mark twice from the left wing against Videoton FC and Sporting Lisbon: in the 80th minute, he delivered a ball for Streller in the 1–0 win over the Hungarians, then provided two assists for Stocker and Degen in the 3–0 win over the Portuguese. These two victories saw Basel make the last sixteen of the competition. They also saw the young number 22's stock rise as he scored two goals in the Swiss cup against FC Locarno before the winter break. These performances were hailed by a nomination for the Golden Boy – the annual award bestowed on the world's most talented young footballer aged under 21 – and the trophy for the Most Promising African Talent of 2012, received during the GLO-CAF awards on 20 December in Accra in Ghana.

'Although he had gone through some difficult spells during the first half of the season, he had already made tremendous progress tactically,' recalls a Basel insider. 'Players with a strong personality like Streller also helped him immerse himself in the culture of FCB, where we like to attack but also to defend. This was felt on the resumption of the league in February, when he could also count on the arrival of his former Arab Contractors teammate Mohamed Elneny. The presence alongside him of his teammate from the Egyptian national side helped him feel freer and he then became one of FCB's most important assets.'

But this was not yet the case in the Swiss domestic league, in which Momo started only five times in the second half of the season, scoring just three goals against Sion, Lucerne and FC Zurich. On the other hand, Murat Yakin had made him one of his weapons of choice in Europe: 'We talk a lot about his pace but little about him on the ball. Salah is one of the smartest players I've ever had the opportunity to coach. He has an incredible ability to stand out and provide his teammates with passes. That proved to be the case against both Tottenham and Chelsea.'

After putting in solid performances against FC Dnipro and Zenit Saint Petersburg, Basel faced Tottenham at home in the second leg of the Europa League quarter-final. It was a historic game and the 36,000 spectators at the St Jakob-Park were convinced their team could do it after coming away with a 2–2 draw in England. Tottenham battled hard and, despite the absence of Gareth Bale, opened the scoring through Clint Dempsey in the 23rd minute. Nil-one. Basel had given themselves plenty of work to do but the response was immediate. Four minutes later, after an interception saw Streller gifted the ball, he served Salah on the right wing, twenty yards from Tottenham's goal. It looked as if his first touch had been too long, but, with two defenders bearing down on him, Mo got the tip of his left foot to the ball and fired it just inside the post of Brad Friedel's goal. One-one.

'He was like an artist with that goal, says a Swiss journalist. 'No wonder he earned the nickname "Picasso". With his talent, a touch of the ball turns into a brushstroke. Salah is capable of giving colour to a move to create a magical painting like he did that night.'

In the end, amid a downpour, Basel went through on penalties after a second 2–2 draw. But Mo Salah had stolen the show and would confirm his promise three weeks later against another English club. At Chelsea, this time Shaqiri's successor distinguished himself in London during the second leg of the semi-final, played on 2 May 2013 at Stamford Bridge. Beaten 2–1 in Switzerland, Yakin's team would have to do it the hard way. Salah gave them hope during stoppage time at the end of the first half: while his team were keeping the Blues' onslaught at bay, the Egyptian international called for a difficult ball at the edge of the area. The pass from his teammate Valentin Stocker was judged to the millimetre, as it needed to be, between two Chelsea defenders Branislav Ivanović and Ryan Bertrand. Momo did not even need to control the ball. He just had to open up his left foot and use the inside of his boot to slide it past the experienced Petr Čech. One-nil. Another work of art! But Chelsea were too much for Basel in the second half, scoring three times thanks to Torres, Moses and David Luiz. The Swiss club saw its dreams of a first European final disappear.

Despite the disappointment, the Rotblau returned to winning ways to collect the Swiss league title in early June. After a narrow victory over Saint-Gall, Basel won their sixteenth domestic title and their fourth in a row. Mohamed Salah lifted his first trophy on European soil. It was enough to brighten up the end of his first season in Basel, marked by a Europa League semi-final and an individual record of ten goals and eleven assists in 50 official matches. He probably thought he could do a lot better, but Mo Salah had already made an impression with a few flashes of brilliance. He ended the season as he had begun it: shining in a national team shirt. Although he was not yet completely untouchable at Basel, he had become indispensable back in Egypt. On 9 and 16 June 2013, he was imperious in two Africa zone qualifying games for the 2014 World Cup, with a hat-trick and an assist during the 4–2 victory over Zimbabwe and the winning goal against Mozambique. Picasso was inspired once more.

Chapter 9
Already on his way

One look at him in the press conference said it all: his head was lowered and he refused to catch anyone's eye, making his awkwardness clear. Mohamed Salah could have done without this story. Usually so discreet, he was at the centre of a controversy in the early part of the 2013–14 season. He was forced to explain himself just a few days before the second leg of the third Champions League qualifying round between Basel and Maccabi Tel Aviv. Media expectation was high due to the rumour that he and his compatriot Mohamed Elneny were intending to boycott the trip to Israel. The rumour came after the uncompromising comments on social media that had been attributed to Salah ('I won't play against Zionists') and his attitude during the first leg, when he had apparently invented the pretext of having to change his boots to avoid shaking hands with the Maccabi players during the team presentation before kick-off.

'It was a very strange situation in which politics got involved in a football match,' remembers a former Basel player. 'He had been blamed for a message posted online and it had created a real controversy in Israel and Egypt. Old stories and disagreements between the two countries were rehashed and it didn't do anyone any good. In the end, after meeting with President Heusler, Mohamed made the right choice. He knew it was a very important match for our club with a lot at stake in terms of football and finances.'

On 3 August 2013, after the Swiss league game against Saint-Gall (1–1), the Egyptian striker appeared in front of the media to announce his decision: 'I will go to Israel. I will play on Tuesday in Tel Aviv. Firstly, because it's my job and I want to play in the Champions League for my club, and also because it's about sport and that has nothing to do with anything else.'

In the end, it would be resolved on the pitch. Three days later, Mo Salah was impervious to the constant uproar in the small Netanya Stadium in Tel Aviv, where he was whistled every time he touched the ball. He even seemed galvanised by so much hostility and scored his team's second goal against Maccabi with his right foot. 'He showed he was mentally tough by turning the pressure into something positive,' says his former manager Murat Yakin.

The match was a springboard to his future achievements in the Champions League. Unlike the previous season, this time Basel did succeed in breaking through the play-offs barrier by knocking out Ludogorets in the next round; once again the Egyptian international was flawless. During the first leg in Bulgaria, he almost took full responsibility for his team's attack onto his own shoulders by opening the scoring at the start of the game with a diagonal half-volley, then equalising to make it 2–2 with another delicate shot from his left 'paintbrush', before finally winning a penalty, converted by Fabian Schär to give Basel a 4–2 win.

'He gained strength from those European games,' continues Yakin. 'Each time he took on an extra dimension. He must have understood that these matches would give him more exposure than he would get in our league.'

Now feared in the Swiss Super League, in which he scored twice and provided four assists before the end of the autumn, the Basel striker made a particular impression when the Swiss team were reunited with Chelsea. After facing each other in the Europa League semi-final the previous season, this time the two teams had hit the big time of the Champions League, where they were drawn in Group E alongside Schalke 04 and Steaua Bucharest. The first duel took place in the opening group game on 18 September in London. 'It was a seminal match in Salah's career,' claims the Swiss journalist Tim Guillemin. 'At Stamford Bridge, he again showed that he wasn't afraid of the atmosphere in English stadiums, but that it actually helped him play better.'

'He was so much better than everyone else,' confirms Patrick Sauteur, who was one of the 2,000 travelling Swiss fans in attendance that night. 'It was one of his best matches for Basel, and it wasn't like they were playing Lausanne-Sport but one of the biggest clubs in Europe. I realised that night that he wasn't going to stay with us for long and that our president would be able to add a zero to his price tag.'

Mo Salah was no longer the hesitant clumsy player who had arrived in Europe the previous season. He had become a technical leader who was respected and closely guarded by his man-to-man marker Ashley Cole. The England international had already come across the Egyptian the previous year and managed to limit the damage for more than an hour. Chelsea were heading for a narrow victory over the generous Swiss team until the 71st minute, when a move began in the Swiss midfield. Fabian Frei carried the ball with him for about ten yards down the left wing before Behrang Safari sent in a measured cross that was laid off immediately by Delgado for Stocker, who, with a single touch, found Mohamed Salah on the right, seemingly completely forgotten by the Chelsea defence. The number 22 had no hesitation. Without even needing to control the ball, he wrapped his left foot around it perfectly to find the far corner of

Petr Čech's goal. The delicately brushed ball bounced just before crossing the line. Goal! Salah celebrated in the arms of Valentin Stocker, while the Chelsea manager José Mourinho seethed. He had not seen anything yet … In the 80th minute, Salah was off again, charging down the left wing before putting in a wicked cross that took a deflection from David Luiz. From the resulting corner, Stocker wrong-footed Petr Čech with an accurate header at the near post. 2–1. Basel held on and Salah had made the difference in Europe once again.

'That performance opened doors for him,' claims the former sporting director Georg Heitz. 'He was all people were talking about in Switzerland after that and the defenders in our league were all terrified of him. There were lots of Egyptian fans and those from neighbouring countries who started coming to see him play in a Basel shirt.'

Mohamed Salah had become a superstar in the land of the pyramids, where they took great delight in his exploits on European soil. He was also exceeding expectations with the Pharaohs. He had scored in the first two games of the season with his national side: against Uganda in a friendly and then against Guinea in the final group qualifier for the World Cup. Brazil, where the finals would be played in the summer of 2014, was no longer so far out of reach for Bob Bradley's team. They had one more hoop to jump through: a two-leg play-off against the formidable team from Ghana, semi-finalists at the last Africa Cup of Nations. But on 15 October 2013, Egypt fell to one of the heaviest defeats in their history. They sank completely in the electric atmosphere of the Baba Yara Sports Stadium in Kumasi and went down by six goals to one. Despite winning a penalty, like his teammates, the match seemed to completely pass Mo Salah by. The jolt of pride that came a month later in Cairo could not erase the disappointment suffered in Ghana. Despite the 2–1 win at the 30 June Stadium, the Basel striker saw his dreams of a first World Cup vanish.

'The elimination affected him badly because he really wanted to help Egypt qualify for the World Cup for the third time in their history,' (after 1936 and 1990) remembers a former teammate. 'It was a huge disappointment but he still managed to put his frustration aside to keep performing for his club.'

It was time for the second act against Chelsea on 26 November 2013. After losing to Schalke 04 and securing two draws against Steaua Bucharest, Basel would have to pull off something amazing against the London team to be in with a hope of qualifying for the Champions League last sixteen. And it was on the genius of their number 22 that the Swiss club would rely yet again for this unlikely dream. In the 87th minute, as the commentator was taking his time describing the English team's substitution of the Brazilian Willian by the young Belgian midfielder Kevin De Bruyne, Basel launched one of their final attacks in what had so far been a goalless game; this was the moment chosen by Fabian Schär to fire a long ball out of defence down the left wing, some 40 yards or so inside the opposition's half. Mohammed Salah ran at full pelt with Ivanović hot on his heels: after controlling the ball and putting the Serbian defender out of position, he used the tip of his left foot to prevent Gary Cahill from coming back at him before unleashing a diagonal shot over someone who was now becoming his victim of choice, Petr Čech. In just three touches, Picasso had the St Jakob-Park jumping with his latest masterpiece. 'Despite the freezing cold, the quality of the opposition and the stakes, he had put one over on Chelsea yet again,' recalls Murat Yakin. 'His third goal against the Blues earned him the nickname of the Egyptian Messi and from that moment on his status changed.'

Anderlecht, Lyon and Tottenham had made an initial approach in the summer of 2013. From now on, the contenders would be much more prestigious and, most importantly, would have better financial weapons at their disposal; they included Inter Milan, Monaco, Manchester United, Liverpool, Juventus, Bayern Munich and Wolfsburg. Interest seems to intensify even further after comments made by the player in the Swiss newspaper *Blick* three days after the 1–0 win over Chelsea: 'It's great to be praised like that, I love those kind of matches. I hope to play in England one day. I want to play for one of the best teams in the world. My favourite clubs are Real Madrid, Manchester United and Chelsea.'

'When he came to us, he knew Basel would only be a stepping stone in his career,' suggests Georg Heitz. 'He always wanted more because he was very ambitious. During the first few months, when he was a substitute, he would come and see me in my office every week and tell me with a smile in broken English "I want to speak with you." It had become a game. We had a good relationship and he wouldn't think twice about coming to talk to me and ask if there had been any offers for him. I would say: "Momo, be patient. It'll take time but it will happen eventually." And we did have offers lined up in the end. German clubs were on the lookout, but it was hard for them to compete with English clubs. Liverpool were very interested and the manager Brendan Rodgers even came to see him play in the Champions League. Then Chelsea joined the negotiations and it was very tight for nearly two months.'

The end of 2013 would prove to be intense for Mohammed Salah: on 1 December, he scored two goals in a single league game for the first time, both in just four minutes on the Young Boys' pitch in Bern (2–2). On 2 December, he received the Golden Player trophy for the best player in the Swiss league during the 2012–13 season but the kiss on the cheek he was given by the award's female presenter would cause a scandal on Egyptian social media. 'They have spoiled my joy. The video shows I was embarrassed. God knows I didn't want that,' said the player afterwards while defending himself on the Arabic language TV channel, Al-Hayat 2. On 11 December, Basel were beaten 2–0 by Schalke 04 and denied the knock-out stages of the Champions League. On 14 December, he played his 79th and last official match for Basel (twenty goals and seventeen assists), with 30 minutes of play at the St Jakob-Park against Lucerne. On 18 December, he was wearing a black suit, white shirt and carefully knotted black bow-tie for his wedding to Magi Mohammed Sadiq, who was dressed all in white. The two had met when they were kids and attended the same school in Nagrig. Their long-lasting and low-key romance eventually ended in marriage. The ceremony brought several celebrities to Cairo, including the new Egyptian national team manager Shawky Gharieb and the internationals Elneny, Kahraba and Zika. The couple set off immediately afterwards for a honeymoon on the shores of the Red Sea but the question had still to be answered: what colour would the Egyptian be wearing at his next club, red or blue?

'Liverpool had made an initial offer of €8 million, which was not enough,' says Georg Heitz. 'We weren't just going to give away our best player. The presence of Chelsea had raised the stakes, so much so that by January, the two clubs had almost reached the same figure. Momo preferred Liverpool but a phone call ended up making him change his mind.'

'José Mourinho called me in person,' Salah would reveal

shortly afterwards. 'It was a long conversation. He told me I was a player he needed, and that I would have an important role. He also told me that Chelsea's style of play would suit me. That was why I picked Chelsea. I had waited over three months for Liverpool.'

On 23 January 2014, the English club made the transfer for a sum of €16.5 million official. Before flying to London to meet his new team, Mohammed Salah reaped his last rewards in Switzerland: he was voted Super League player of the year at the SFL Award Night and the fans' favourite player for 2013. Although he was not present in Lucerne to receive the trophies, he did not forget to say goodbye to his teammates: 'He thanked us for everything we had done for him and we wished him all the best for the future,' remembers the goalkeeper Germano Vailati. 'We were going to miss his talent as well as his sense of humour.'

Chapter 10

Chelsea

'Did I play with him? Let's just say he played a little bit with me. He was 21 and José Mourinho was really hard on him' These remarks were made by Samuel Eto'o. Like the majority of the Blues' players between 2014 and 2015, the Cameroon striker wondered how Mohamed Salah could have failed to make a name for himself during his first spell in English football. If truth be told, with hindsight, his two half seasons in a Chelsea shirt looked like a complete disaster.

When the London club came to an agreement with the Egyptian prodigy in January 2014, to the great displeasure of Liverpool – one of their direct competitors for the Premier League title, alongside Manchester United – Mourinho seemed delighted at the prospect of welcoming the Basel player: 'He's young, he's fast, he's creative, he's enthusiastic. When we analysed him he looks like the kind of humble personality on the pitch, ready to work for the team,' explained the 'Special One.'

After his official presentation, the former Arab Contractors star took over the number 15 shirt from Kevin de Bruyne, who had been sold to the German club VfL Wolfsburg for just over €20 million a few days earlier. But despite the departure of the young Belgian, as well as that of Juan Mata to Manchester United, competition for the four attacking positions was extremely fierce. Salah would have to compete with eight players: the Brazilians

Willian, Oscar and Ramires, the Belgian Eden Hazard, the former Barça and Inter Milan star Samuel Eto'o, as well as the Spaniard Fernando Torres, the German André Schürrle and the Senegalese Demba Ba. 'We knew it was going to be very tough for him to carve out a role for himself in the squad that had about 30 top-level players,' remembers a Salah insider. 'He was coming from a league that people in England didn't think much of and the controversy over what had happened with Maccabi Tel Aviv hadn't given him a good image internationally. He was starting off with a big handicap, but Mohamed was ready for this new challenge.'

After coming on at the end of two Premier League games in February against Newcastle United and West Bromwich Albion, followed by a start at the beginning of the second half against Manchester City during the last sixteen elimination from the FA Cup, Mohamed Salah soon grasped that he was not going to be one of his new manager's first choices and that he was going to have to fight to get time on the pitch. But it would take more than that to discourage the 21-year-old striker. In early March, during his first interview with *Chelsea Magazine*, he spoke confidently about making his mark in the British capital: 'London is a very nice city. This move is a fantastic thing for me – going to a big team like this is fantastic for anyone – and I hope I can play here for a long time and have a good career. I know it will not be easy to play every game for Chelsea because we have so many very good players in my position, but I hope to show how hard I work and then we will see. I hope I can now start to score for Chelsea, not against Chelsea.'

And Mo Salah kept his promise. Ten days later, on 22 March 2014 at Stamford Bridge, he finally scored his first goal for his new team during a demonstration against Arsenal (6–0). After coming on in place of Oscar in the 67th minute,

'Picasso' attracted plenty of attention with his first touch by slotting the ball past the post of the opposing keeper Wojciech Szczęsny with his left foot for the Blues' final goal in what would be a historic derby. The Egyptian beamed as he went to congratulate the teammate who had provided the assist, Nemanja Matić. He had been waiting for that moment for almost two months. It was the spark before the flame, as on 5 April, the 33rd matchday of the Premier League season, Salah stood out once again in his new back garden in the Royal Borough. Lining up in his favourite position on the right wing alongside Willian, Schürrle and Torres, the player recruited during the January transfer window offered up his most impressive performance in a Chelsea shirt.

In the 32nd minute, he confirmed his understanding with Matić by taking advantage of another assist from the Serb to wrong-foot the Stoke keeper. He kissed the green turf and gave a thumbs up in thanks to his manager. Salah had redis-covered his ease and the confidence he had become accus-tomed to during his exploits with Basel on the European stage. During the second half, he darted down the left wing and forced a foul from Wilkinson just inside the box. Frank Lampard converted the penalty on the rebound. 2–0. Salah took advantage of the end of the game to put the finishing touches to his all-out persuasion campaign. In the 72nd min-ute, this time it was Willian who was put through by the number 15 on the edge of the box for a third goal scored by the Brazilian playmaker with a surfeit of finesse. Fans at the London club were won over. José Mourinho was jubilant: 'Salah is the type of player we need because we have wingers who prefer to play with the ball at their feet. He's the type of player who prefers the ball in space. Chelsea did very well to bring him. We know he needs time, we know next season he will be an important player for us.'

Although by the time May 2014 rolled around, Chelsea finished third in the English league behind Manchester United and Liverpool, Mohamed Salah took advantage of the last five games of the season to string together a series of starts and finish off his half-season at the Blues with eleven appearances, two goals and two assists. 'He now felt important in the team because Mourinho was finally giving him the best conditions in which to succeed,' the insider continues. 'Also, before he went off on holiday, he had been decisive for the national side against Chile and Jamaica [one goal and one assist]. It was a good omen for the future and we were already imagining that he was going to make a name for himself with the Blues.'

But that would not be the case. The last six months of 2014 could be summed up with a succession of footballing disappointments. The tone was set from the start of pre-season training in July, with the revelations broken by the *Kingfut* news outlet: 'The Egyptian minister could force Mohamed Salah to return to Egypt to carry out his military service lasting between one and three years. His registration in an education programme that would allow him to travel has been rescinded.'

'Mohamed has expressed shock about the decision,' reported the national team director Ahmed Hassan. 'When I spoke to him on the phone, he told me he is trying to represent Egypt in the best way possible. Is this the best response from the country?' Fortunately, the case was settled in three days by the federation and the ministry, and the Egyptian international was officially released from his military obligations on 21 July.

This scare was accompanied by the emergence of the first few questions. Was it really likely Mourinho would make him a cast-iron certainty in the starting eleven next season? Salah was entitled to be doubtful given how active Chelsea had been on the transfer market. The Blues had been recruiting heavily upfront: the Ivorian Didier Drogba, the Frenchman Loïc Rémy and especially the Spanish internationals Diego Costa and Cesc Fábregas, who had been brought in over the summer to strengthen an area of the pitch from which only Demba Ba and Fernando Torres had left. Despite scoring in pre-season games against Wimbledon and the Dutch team Vitesse Arnhem, the former Basel player was soon relegated to the bottom of the list of attacking solutions: between August and October, he played in only five official games and had to content himself with a pitiful twelve minutes play in the league, six minutes in the Champions League and only two starts in the EFL Cup against Bolton and Shrewsbury Town. It was a poor record for a player who had been heralded as a future superstar just a few months earlier!

'We were wondering how he was going to get himself out of it,' admits a former Chelsea player. 'Mourinho was well known for piling up young players and being uncompromising with them. Kevin De Bruyne and Romelu Lukaku had paid the price in previous seasons and it was happening again with Mo Salah and André Schürrle. People were suddenly questioning why the Portuguese coach had recruited Mohamed in the first place. Did he really want to see him blossom under his management or was it more about getting one over on Liverpool, as had been the case before, in 2013, with Tottenham for Willian?'

The tone of the comments coming from the 'Special One' had certainly changed. Protective and benevolent for the first six months, José Mourinho now seemed to have distanced himself from his African star. He even had no qualms about making a public dig at him in late October. The Portuguese manager was unhappy with the attitude of several of his players during the snatched last sixteen League Cup win against the Third Division team Shrewsbury Town (2–1). Despite an assist for Drogba to open the scoring, Salah found himself in the firing line: 'I expect people that are not playing a lot to raise the level, to create problems for me,' Mourinho told the waiting microphones after the game. 'I love problems. I love problems of choice. But after tonight it will be easy to choose my team for Saturday. Did Salah and Schürrle disappoint me? Yes!'

28 October 2014 marked a turning point, almost like a point of no return. The Egyptian would barely play again: a single start on 10 December in the Champions League in a meaningless game against Sporting Lisbon and about fifteen minutes against Tottenham in the Premier League on 1 January 2015. More often than not, he was also absent from the team sheet. He eventually asked for a meeting with his manager in early January. 'Salah was frank with Mourinho during that discussion,' claims a Chelsea insider. 'He told him how unhappy he was and that he didn't have enough opportunities to play or to be able to show his potential. He also said he wanted to leave and that he had received some enquiries from other clubs.'

Several English teams were in fact keen to pick up the Chelsea player on loan; Sunderland, Stoke City, Everton and Queens Park Rangers had got the sniff of a bargain. 'Even though a few weeks earlier, Mourinho had assured him that there was no question of him leaving and that if he needed to move he would only be moving house, the Blues now looked more favourably on him leaving. English teams were an option, but in the end he served as a bargaining chip in the transfer of the Colombian Juan Cuadrado.'

Almost a year to the day after arriving in London, Mo Salah was packing his bags again. After Switzerland and

England, the Egyptian star would continue his tour of Europe a little further south, in Italy, on a six-month loan to Fiorentina.

Before hanging up his blue shirt, he played one last game for Chelsea in the FA Cup against Bradford City (2–4) on 24 January 2015. As a farewell gift to the fans at Stamford Bridge, he provided one last assist to the Brazilian Ramires in his nineteenth and last official game for the Blues. The adventure had ended, well short of his expectations. But despite it all, he was not ready to forget his spell in London: in a year, he had discovered how demanding top-flight football could be and experienced a competitive Premier League dressing room. He had also matured and grown up, with the arrival of his first child, a little girl named Makka, after the holy site of Mecca in Saudi Arabia. She was born in October 2014 in the maternity unit at the Kensington Wing.

Chapter 11

The Egyptian campaign

It fell to Vincenzo Guerini, the midfielder and coach-turned-club manager, to introduce the new arrival on 6 February 2015. Mohamed Salah had landed in Florence two days earlier, welcomed by journalists and fans who wasted no time putting a purple scarf around his neck. On the official ACF Fiorentina Facebook page, the likes ran into their thousands, as did the posts in Arabic. 'I'm Egyptian, I'm 22 and I'm looking for a girlfriend in Florence. With Salah, Florence is my city,' wrote one. 'Florence was already famous all over the world, now it will be even more so,' predicted another. 'Montella, if you pick Salah, Fiorentina will have 20 million new fans straight away,' said a third. The Egyptian community, which, according to official estimates, numbered 135,000 people in 2014, the eighth largest among non-EU citizens in Italy, had mobilised for the arrival of the Pharaoh. And it was not only immigrants: messages flooded in from Egypt, Palestine and Syria. After so much time on the bench at Chelsea, everyone was longing to see Mo on the pitch, wearing the purple strip. The event was so hotly anticipated that Egyptian television screened a documentary about Salah's career the night before his official presentation and broadcast the press conference live on the big day itself. At 2pm on 6 February, the Egyptian Messi was presented for the approval of the local and national media in the Sala Manuela Righini at the Artemio Franchi Stadium. Wearing the club suit, with a lily on his jacket pocket and a purple tie, a smiling Mo seemed relaxed in front of the flashing cameras, showing off his new number 74 shirt, a tribute to the victims of the Port Said riot. After the photographers had got their shots, Guerini introduced the new Viola striker: 'You know about the negotiations. He's a player with a bright future ahead of him. He has a very high release clause, which means Chelsea really believe in him. We hope he settles quickly into a dressing room that has accepted him in the best way possible. We want to welcome him and give him all the help he needs because it's never easy to come from where he's come from and to join a team in January, halfway through the season.'

He then opened the floor for questions.

'This is a time when the great champions of Italian football are going abroad, especially to England, but here's someone who's decided to come from Chelsea to Florence. How did this choice come about?'

Mo listened to the translation and answered in Arabic. 'The Italian league is played at a very high level, which is why I chose to come here. I think the players who are leaving Italy are doing so to broaden their horizons and gain experience. Before I came to Florence I spoke to Ahmed Hegazy [an Egyptian central defender who spent three seasons at Fiorentina] and he told me great things about the city, the team and the atmosphere. I hope to stay for as long as possible. I want to win the league, and not just once. I don't intend to go back to Chelsea. I hope to grow and improve at Fiorentina, with the whole team.'

He was then asked if there were any Italian players he admired: 'Of course. Lots of Serie A players have been role models for me. Like Batistuta, Baggio, Totti and Del Piero.'

'Do you want to say anything about what's happening in the Arab world at the moment?' asked one journalist.

'I'm a footballer. I don't talk about politics.' After getting his fingers burned by the Maccabi affair and the controversy that followed, Salah smiled and kept silent. He preferred to talk about football, reassuring the auditorium about his role and keenness: 'At Basel and Chelsea I played in a 4-3-3 formation, on the right or left wing or as a second striker.'

'Is there a chance you'll play on Sunday?' 'I hope to be ready for Sunday. My aim is always to play.'

Sunday 8 February, the 22nd matchday of the season, saw a lunchtime kick-off at the Franchi. On a beautiful sunny day, Vincenzo Montella's Fiorentina faced Stefano Colantuono's Atalanta. Mohamed Salah came on for Joaquín in the 65th minute, with the score locked at 1–1. He made his Serie A debut in a game that ended in a 3–2 win for the team in purple. Montella talked about the new arrival in the post-match press conference: 'He's a dynamic player. He gave us pace and energy. He's great when we're in possession but he needs to improve his defensive work.' It became clear that the manager, known as 'Aeroplanino' during his playing career, rated the Egyptian when he put him in the starting eleven away at Sassuolo for the 23rd match of the season on 14 February. In a white shirt with the Save the Children logo, Momo wore a black armband. With the permission of the Lega Calcio, it was a tribute to the 25 victims of the clashes between police and the White Knights outside Cairo's Air Defense Stadium before the game between Zamalek and ENPPI on 7 February.

The match in Reggio Emilia kicked off. With less than a minute played, Salah took advantage of a long ball to fly down the left wing and put in a diagonal shot that troubled but failed to beat Andrea Consigli. It was the first demonstration of what he could do. Thirty minutes into the first half, a back-heel from Khouma Babacar freed the purple number 74, who left two defenders in his wake and this time beat the advancing Sassuolo keeper with his left foot. It was his first Serie A goal. Not content, a few minutes later, he returned the favour and gifted an exquisite ball to Babacar.

This was just the beginning … there was no stopping the boy from Nagrig now. In less than a month he scored six goals in seven games. Those who thought Mourinho's loan was a dud had to think again. Salah was not like Wallace Oliveira dos Santos, Van Ginkel or Marko Marin, whom the Special One had sent to Inter and Fiorentina. Those who were wondering whether the Egyptian could replace Cuadrado 'The Vespa' could not deny the facts. Around Florence, people were joking: 'Cuadrado who?'

Unlike the Colombian, who had taken twelve games in purple to find the back of the net, the number 74 scored immediately. Over and over again. And they were important goals. Three on target in the league (against Torino and Inter, following the one against Sassuolo), a decisive strike in the Europa League against Tottenham and two in the Coppa Italia against Juventus. They were worth talking about.

The second leg of the Europa League last sixteen was played at the Franchi Stadium on 26 February. The Viola had secured a 1–1 draw in England. Mario Gómez took care of giving Fiorentina the lead in the 54th minute. Fed the perfect ball by Milan Badelj, the German bomber made no mistake in front of Lloris. Seven minutes later, Salah found himself in a one-on-one with Spurs' French keeper, but fired it right at him. He would get another opportunity in the 71st minute: Momo picked up the ball to the right of the London team's box and pulled off a one-two with Gómez by the goal line to get the ball back. Jan Vertonghen appeared to have the better of him, but the Egyptian persisted, stubbornly taking the ball off him and unleashing a strike that flew past Lloris. He pulled off his shirt and ran to the *curva* to celebrate. It earned him a caution, but what did a yellow card matter for a goal that saw his team qualify for the quarter-finals? The press awarded Mo's performance an eight out of ten, and not just for the goal but 'for his shots just on the edge of the offside trap and his darting runs with the ball at his feet that were a constant worry for the Tottenham defence and opened up huge holes for his teammates.' It was not just the Italian press that sang Salah's praises; the British press also had their say. With plenty of irony, as the *Guardian* pointed out the fact that the 'chief tormentor' of Pochettino's men 'is still a Chelsea player, on loan from the West London club as part of the deal in which Juan Cuadrado departed Florence this winter.' Or they took aim at the Special One, like the *Telegraph*: 'Mohamed Salah, deemed not good enough by José Mourinho, produced a killer goal to end Spurs' hopes.'

The confirmation that Mourinho had made a mistake in letting him go came on 1 March at the San Siro against Inter, the Portuguese manager's former team. Salah came on suddenly for the injured Babacar in the 43rd minute. He made such an immediate impact that two Nerazzurro defenders, Nemanja Vidić and Juan Jesus, earned themselves yellow cards. Losing their heads at the back, Roberto Mancini's team conceded a goal to the number 74. A cross was put in by Pasqual as Handanović came out, leaving the ball in the middle of the area; Mo did not miss the open goal. It was the Egyptian's fourth, the goal that gave the Viola their first win over Inter at the San Siro in fifteen years. On the team's return from Milan, the Florentine fans welcomed Momo with the song that now rang out across the stands at the Franchi: '*Siam venuti fin qua, siam venuti fin qua per vedere segnare Salah*' (We've come here, we've come here to see Salah score).

And Salah did indeed continue to score: two extraordinary goals against Fiorentina's traditional rivals Juventus in the first leg of the Coppa Italia semi-final in Turin on 5 March. In the eleventh minute, the Viola defence cleared a corner from Pepe as Mo picked up the ball, sprinted for 75 yards, outfoxed the Bianconero full-back and fired the ball past Marco Storari. Juve reacted and equalised through Fernando Llorente, whose header went in off the bottom of the post, but there was more to come. Marchisio lost the ball; Salah capitalised and sped into the box to steal his second of the night. Two-one to the Viola. The Old Lady had not lost at home in almost two years, since 10 April 2013 against Bayern Munich. The final of the Coppa seemed like a foregone conclusion, but Fiorentina were overwhelmed in the second leg. The European dream also vanished. The Viola were soundly beaten by Seville (5–0 over both legs) in the semi-final in May. They finished fourth in the table but it was enough to earn them European qualification. Mohammed Salah ended his three and a half months in the Renaissance city with 26 appearances and nine goals. Six in Serie A (the last three against Sampdoria, Empoli and Parma), two in the Coppa Italia and one in Europe.

Numbers aside, the boy from Nagrig had, just like he promised, won over the heart of a city like Florence, which was still living with the memories of Antognoni, Baggio, Batigol and Rui Costa. He had won its heart with his long runs down the wing, dribbling sequences, goals, prayers and apparent respectability. The Florentine fans had fallen in love with him. And his compatriots in Tuscany had made him their idol. In February, after Momo's first goal against Sassuolo, they organised a party in an Egyptian restaurant on Via del Palazzuolo. Someone explained: 'If Salah scores, it's a great sign of integration for us. We can't help but be happy.' In March, Momo took to social media to share a picture of the inscription that had been cut into the wooden front door of the building where he lived in central Florence, near the Ponte Vecchio.

It simply said 'Salah', above a large heart pierced by an arrow. Florence loved him and did not want the object of its affections to get away. But after everything he had shown on the pitches of Serie A, Salah was the object of desire for clubs, both in Italy and further afield: Inter, AC Milan, Juve, Roma, Atlético Madrid and Wolfsburg, to name but a few. A fight broke out over Momo, the likes of which had not been seen in Italy for years. The Della Valles, Diego and Andrea, owners of Fiorentina since 2002, were keen to hold onto their player. They saw him as the cornerstone around which to build the footballing project designed by Paulo Sousa, the Portuguese manager who had taken over from Montella. They paid Chelsea €1 million to extend the loan to the 2015–16 season. Then they attempted to come to a financial agreement with the player, offering his entourage €3 million for four years plus bonuses, compared with €800,000 the previous season. It was described by Guerini as an 'insane' offer.

And that was not all; they were also prepared, in agreement with Chelsea, to buy the player outright for a sum of around €18 million. It would be a significant investment for the club, which, given the forward was only 23, they hoped would pay off in the future in terms of opening up other markets, in addition to the attributes he brought. Salah's response was all that was needed. Andrea Della Valle, the club's honorary president, was optimistic, convinced that they could meet the player's requests. Days passed and no word came from Momo, who was on holiday. Meetings continued between the club and his representatives, without anything concrete. And then the ultimatum came: Salah would need to decide if he was going to accept Fiorentina's offer by 8pm on 2 July. Silence. And that was the last straw. Confirmation came courtesy of Ramy Abbas, the lawyer who takes care of Salah's interests: 'We've decided not to stay at Fiorentina.

Mohamed will move to another Italian club this summer.'
Everything indicated that his probable destination would be
Mancini's Inter, who had allegedly approached the player, in
contravention of the rules, to try to convince him to join the
Nerazzurri. On Sunday 5 July, the front page of *La Gazzetta
dello Sport* read: 'Showdown over Salah. Chelsea say yes to
Inter but Fiorentina warn them off. After coming to an agreement with the Egyptian, the Nerazzurri press the London
club for 20 million. Is it a done deal? No. Fiorentina com-
plain: "You approached a player under contract."' *Il Corriere
dello Sport* added: 'Storm clouds over Salah. Florence accuse
Inter!' The boy from Nagrig was back on the front page
the following day: 'The Egyptian campaign. Salah transfer.
Fiorentina and Inter in war of words through tweets and press
releases. A Florentine advisor says (in a personal capacity)
that Inter should be relegated to Serie B. Meanwhile, Roma
are waiting in the wings,' read the headline in *La Gazzetta.*

Inter were not the only front on which the Della Valles
were fighting. They were also at loggerheads with Salah. They
retracted the 'insane' offer, called him up for the pre-season
training camp at Moena on 13 July and instructed their law-
yers to 'assess the actions required to protect the rights of
the club.' Momo had his say in some tweets: 'Rumours in the
media should not always be believed. I respect Fiorentina
and I don't want to talk right now.' And then: 'Thanks for
respecting me.' Nothing more. The saga of the summer
continued, but the sticking point between the Florentine
club and the player was leaked: when the contract was being
drawn up with Fiorentina, Salah asked for a private agreement that would allow him to leave in June if an offer arrived
from another club.

'We used the documents drawn up between the parties in
January,' explained Abbas. 'The contract with Fiorentina has

already expired, so we're going back to Chelsea; we're wait-ing for new offers for him to come in. Any new offers, as well as any improved offers from Fiorentina, have been rejected by the player. The situation was clear back in February and they've been aware of it all along. Fiorentina is a big club, and, like all big clubs, they know what they're signing and what they're getting into. Is money the issue? Finances are only a small part of it; opportunities that are better for his career could also come his way. Would Salah go to another Italian club? The only thing I can say is at the moment he's a Chelsea player, but there have been other offers of course, both from Italy and abroad. We'll decide on his future in a couple of days.'

As far as the Colombian lawyer was concerned, the situ-ation was crystal clear and the saga would soon be resolved, without dragging on. Given the hornets' nest that had been stirred up, Inter and Roma seemed to take a step back, for the moment at least. Roberto Mancini explained in a press conference: 'Until Salah's situation has been clarified, we can't talk about him. We can't do anything. When he's on the market, we can start talking. You've seen what he's done at Fiorentina in just six months, but at the moment we can't approach him at Inter.' And so it was. Two weeks later, Roma stepped into the ring. Walter Sabatini, the sporting director, who had seen him taken from under his nose in the win-ter transfer window, flew to London to meet with Salah and Abbas at the Zafferano restaurant on the Fulham Road. He offered a four-year deal for €3 million a season. By 23 July it was decided. Momo was virtually a Roma player. In addition to the agreement of the Egyptian striker, who had rejected the final offers from Inter and Napoli, Sabatini had also secured the OK from Chelsea: a loan with a mandatory release clause of around €20 million. Mohamed Salah landed at Fiumicino

Airport at 6.30pm on 29 July. But AS Roma were as yet unable to announce their new purchase and Momo could not sign the new contract as he waited for his transfer. Meanwhile, Fiorentina promised a tough legal battle. And it would go all the way. They lodged a complaint with FIFA against Chelsea and the Egyptian player for breach of contractual agreements. They demanded compensation of €30 million and, if the governing body of world football found in their favour, the player could receive a four-month ban. FIFA rejected Fiorentina's complaint in May 2016 but the Viola did not give up and took their appeal to the Court of Arbitration for Sport in Lausanne. In June 2017, the CAS rejected the appeal and upheld FIFA's decision. The Salah case was closed and Ramy Abbas took to Twitter to lash out at Fiorentina: 'How do you say "clowns" in Italian?' 'And how do you say "purple"?'

The legal case may have dragged on for two years but the sporting case came to an end on 6 August 2015. The statement came at 7pm: 'AS Roma are delighted to confirm the signing of Egyptian international forward Mohamed Salah from Chelsea. The 23 year old has signed a four-year contract with the Giallorossi.'

This was followed by selfies with his new shirt, the number 11, hugs, handshakes and Mo signing his contract for the TV cameras. His second official presentation press conference in less than seven months came the next day. Italo Zanzi, Roma's American CEO, introduced him: 'We're delighted to present Mohamed Salah, a young but very talented player. We're very confident about the future. Welcome to Rome.' The questions began and the Egyptian Messi explained: 'My time at Fiorentina was very useful, very positive. I spent six months there and my family and I were very happy. But that's come to an end now. I had the right to choose and that's why I'm here, at Roma.'

Chapter 12
Caput mundi

Mo hardly had time to get his bearings before having to fly to Valencia for a pre-season friendly. Just days after his official presentation, he took part in the 44th edition of the Orange Trophy at the Mestalla Stadium on 8 August. Salah debuted in a white number 11 shirt and left his calling card. He had already scored by the ninth minute. Captain Francesco Totti put Gervinho through, but finding himself on his own in front of Mathew Ryan, the Ivorian hit the post; despite the open goal, he then hit the other post with the rebound! It was up to Momo to finish the job. The game ended 3–1 in favour of the Giallorossi, who, despite the beating they had taken three days earlier against Barcelona at the Camp Nou, were leaving Spain with some confidence restored.

The final pre-season friendly was scheduled for 14 August at the Stadio Olimpico. The new purchases of Salah and Edin Džeko were officially presented to the fans amidst deafening applause before the team took to the pitch to play Sevilla. Mo chipped the Andalusian keeper to gift the second goal to Džeko and, in the 65th minute, slotted the ball under the crossbar from an angle with a powerful right-footed shot. It was Roma's fifth goal in a game that ended 6–4 to the Giallorossi. The first league game came on 22 August at Hellas Verona, as the number 11 received his captain's blessing. 'He's played for some big clubs,' Totti told Roma TV. 'He's physically strong and has scored a lot of goals for

Fiorentina. He already knows Italian football and we'll help him settle in straight away, even if he doesn't need us to.' If truth be told, despite his exploits over the summer, it did take a while for the Egyptian to settle in. Mo Salah remained silent in front of goal during the first three games of the league season and his Champions League debut against Barcelona. But he showed up big time on 20 September at the Olimpico, against Sassuolo, a team that clearly brought him luck.

'A rare pearl, a masterpiece, a piece of magic, a marvel.' As well as: 'a fantastic, amazing, incredible goal.' The list went on and on. Metaphors and adjectives could not do Salah's first Giallorosso league goal justice. And they were more than just hollow words, given that even Momo himself described it as the goal of his career so far, alongside the one he had scored for Fiorentina against Juve in the Coppa Italia. This 'rare pearl' came after two wasted chances that had seen the number 11 break down the wing but end up shooting straight at Andrea Consigli at the finish. It was definitely a case of third time lucky. After a headed clearance from the Sassuolo defence on the end of a Roma corner, from outside the box Salah hit the bullseye with a shot from the outside of his left foot that flew inside Consigli's right post. It was the team from the capital's second goal after Totti's 300th for the club, earning them a 2–2 draw. Salah had broken his duck and, as had been the case in Florence, once he had scored his first, in keeping with Ruud Van Nistelrooy's pearl of wisdom ('Goals are like ketchup, you try and try and then they all come at once'), more followed. The number 11 scored in Genoa in the defeat to Sampdoria, at home to Carpi, then missed out away to Palermo but bagged his fourth at the Olimpico against Empoli.

By now it was 25 October, the ninth matchday of the league season. Roma faced Fiorentina at the Artemio

Franchi. To get an understanding of the atmosphere the ex-Viola would face, it is worth recalling a few lines of the open letter addressed to Salah by Giuseppe Calabresi in the local Florentine pages of *La Repubblica*: 'In all honesty, we hoped we would never see you again, but now you're coming back to the Franchi as a traitor [...] You fled from Florence after the city had practically adopted you. We pulled you up out of the cellar at Chelsea and gave you an opportunity. You started smiling again with us. You rediscovered the desire to play football. You felt important again. We filled the city with selfies. We cosseted you like a real champion and you, at the first chance you got, you left. You didn't even have the courage to explain, you made others do it. Others who are more arrogant than you. And here we are, together again. You on one side [the wrong side] and us on the other.'

If this was what was being written in the papers, it was not difficult to imagine the fans and the atmosphere in the stadium. So much so that Rudi Garcia, Roma's manager, had been suggesting all week that Momo would not play. But in the end he did include the Egyptian in the starting line-up. The whistling began during the warm-up. And there was more. Banners aimed at the Giallorossi's number 11 – some ironic, others less so – filled the stands: 'Salahme', 'Salah Beduino', '– Kebab + Lampredotti', a reference to the typical Florentine sandwich made from a cow's stomach. The boy from Nagrig seemed not to notice and broke the deadlock in the sixth minute. After a one-two with Miralem Pjanić on the right wing, he unleashed a swerving shot with his left foot from the edge of the box that ended up in the bottom corner of the Florentine goal. He then timidly raised his arms and showed his palms. He did not want to celebrate in front of an audience he had won over only a few months earlier. But the gesture was not enough to appease the fans,

who had never looked kindly on former players, as Roberto
Baggio and Gabriel Batistuta could attest; this became clear
when, in the 87th minute, Salah was cautioned for a tussle
with Facundo Roncaglia, reacted angrily towards the referee and was consequently sent off. His exit from the pitch
was met with boos from the stands and he was later given a
one-match ban. But in the meantime Roma were top of the
table with twenty points, two ahead of Napoli. *Il Corriere dello
Sport*, with statistics to hand, sang the praises of the Egyptian:
'Salah has already gone down in Roma's history books. His
impact for the club from the capital has been devastating, as
demonstrated by the five goals he has scored in the first nine
matches of the league season. Since the Second World War,
only Gabriel Omar Batistuta has scored more than Salah
in their first nine games for the Giallorossi. The Argentine
bomber, wrestled from Fiorentina for 70 billion lire in the
summer of 2000, scored nine goals in his first nine games.'

To make sure he lived up to this, Salah also scored in
the Champions League, a competition he loved and one of
the reasons why he chose Roma. On 4 November against
Bayern Leverkusen (3–2 to the Giallorossi), he scored the
fastest goal in the club's European Cup history. One minute
and 40 seconds to be precise. Just onside, Džeko put Salah
through and he sped away, beating a hesitant Leno with the
outside of his left foot. It was a shame the number 11's positive run had to come to an abrupt end four days later in the
Rome derby: Mo went off on a stretcher in the 58th minute
after a nasty tackle by Senad Lulić, Lazio's Bosnian defender.
'It'll be a miracle if he hasn't broken his ankle,' said an angry
Rudi Garcia. It would turn out to be a partial rupture of the
outer lateral ankle ligament: 28 days out, four games missed.
Mo made his return 9 December for the final Champions
League Group E game against Bate Borisov, coming on for

Iturbe in the fourteenth minute of the second half. The game ended in a goalless draw. Garcia's team had been disappointing and were whistled as they left the pitch at the Olimpico, but qualified for the last sixteen, second in their group behind Barcelona, who had torn apart the Romans 6–1 at the Camp Nou.

At Christmas, Momo was interviewed for the club's official website. The fans asked the questions and he answered.

Why did you choose Roma?
'For several reasons. I want to win something here. I like the city and I like the club. I like everything. I'm happy.'

What's your favourite Italian dish?
'I like pasta with tomato sauce, and risotto.'

What would you like to improve in your playing style?
'I would like to improve my shots from outside the box, using my right foot more and my headed game. As well as playing faster.'

Why did you choose the number 11?
'Because I like it. I didn't want an unusual number. There weren't that many choices and I couldn't choose the same number I play with for Egypt because obviously, the number 10 wasn't available!' (Totti, the club captain, was the number 10).

Do you have a message for young Egyptian footballers?
'You have to dream, that's all I can say. Believe in yourselves, trust in what you are. Fight to achieve your goals. Never think you're not good enough. Believe and give everything you have: if you do, I'm sure you can achieve anything you want.'

Apart from football, what's your favourite sport?
'It's not a sport, but I would say the PlayStation.'

Are you better at football with the ball at your feet or at
PlayStation?
'Much better at PlayStation!'

As well as PlayStation, Mohamed Salah also liked fishing, or so it seemed. On 28 December, during the winter break, he posted a photo on Twitter of him on a boat out at sea, proudly showing off a big fish he had just caught. He was not doing quite so well at snagging goals though. Since his injury, Momo no longer seemed like the player who had captivated both Florence and Rome. His performances had been below par and he seemed to have little desire to dribble or amaze, going eight games without scoring. The Roma fans had to wait until Momo's lucky team Sassuolo came around to see him find his feet again in front of goal. Sassuolo again! On 2 February 2016 in Reggio Emilia, Salah got things started with the goal of the season's 23rd round of matches, at least as far as the fans asked by the Serie A league were concerned: spinning around with his left foot on the edge of the area, he fired the ball past Consigli. The final score was 2–0. It was a breath of fresh air for the Giallorossi and for Luciano Spalletti, the Tuscan from Certaldo, who had taken over from Rudi Garcia on the Roma bench on 14 January.

8 March 2016, the Santiago Bernabéu Stadium; the second leg of the Champions League last sixteen. In the first leg, Roma had been powerless against Zinedine Zidane's Real Madrid. Two-nil to the Blancos with goals from Cristiano Ronaldo and Jesé. Overturning the result in the Merengues' own backyard seemed like mission impossible. But hope springs eternal. While Real were relying on Cristiano 'El

Bicho', who had scored four of the seven goals Madrid had put past Celta de Vigo that weekend, Roma were counting on Salah, who had scored twice against Fiorentina in the Giallorossi's 4–1 win. Ronaldo and Salah were both in good form, so much so that *France Football* had included the pair in its European best eleven of the weekend. But it was to be Cristiano who would dominate on his home turf at the Bernabéu. As Džeko and Salah faltered, the Portuguese player was unforgiving. He sank the Italians' dreams of glory in just four minutes. In the 64th minute, Lucas Vázquez sped off down the right wing leaving Lucas Digne behind, before crossing into the middle, where the Portuguese player beat Kostas Manolas to the ball and scored. In the 68th minute, the white number 7 went on a run before providing James Rodríguez with an assist the Colombian didn't think twice about, scoring with a diagonal shot to make it 2–0. All the Roma fans were left with was the scant consolation of a standing ovation dedicated by their Madrid counterparts to Francesco Totti as he stepped onto the pitch. Roma were out; Real would go on to win the Champions League in Milan against Atlético Madrid.

The Giallorossi had little to hearten them at the end of their season. They had kissed goodbye to the Coppa Italia in December, losing on penalties to Spezia in the last sixteen. They had finished third in the league, behind Juventus and Napoli, worse than the previous season when they had grabbed second behind the Old Lady. But they had secured a Champions League spot for the coming year. Mohamed Salah ended his Serie A season on 13 May with a goal at the San Siro against AC Milan (3–1 to the Giallorossi). His tally reached fifteen goals (fourteen in Serie A and one in the Champions League) and six assists. He was Roma's top scorer. And he was not quite done because, on 20 May at the Hazza bin Zayed Stadium in Al Ain, the fourth largest city in the United Arab Emirates, he scored again against Al Ahly, the Cairo team for whom he had dreamt of playing just a few years earlier. He was the undisputed star of the trip: TV cameras, microphones, flashes, selfies and autograph requests just kept on coming. Not even Francesco Totti was as popular as the number 11 in that part of the world. The captain admitted: 'I didn't expect such a warm welcome in Dubai, it was really nice to see. It was also great for me to make so many friends.'

The night before the game, the Roma manager Spalletti said: 'We came here to play this friendly because of Salah, but we're delighted. Will I take an interest in any of the Al Ahly players? Well, having seen what Mohamed can do, I'd take another four or five like him!' joked the coach, with a hint of seriousness. He really valued his young Egyptian, as the following story demonstrates ... On 26 February 2016, before the Empoli-Roma game, Spalletti arrived at the Trigoria training ground with a surprise: a video of Roma's 5–0 win over Palermo five days earlier. Thirty minutes into the second half, with the score at 4–0 and after having already scored twice, Momo Salah chased an opponent for 50 yards into the Giallorosso area to get the ball off him. 'What you see here is a behaviour that's crazy in its beauty. You've taken the piss out of me for years when I've tried to tell you about the right kind of behaviour. This is the right kind of behaviour!'

His manager was not the only one who doted on Momo. AS Roma opened a Twitter account in Arabic for him. So as not to make things awkward for him, they asked the Lega Calcio if the ballkids rather than the players could hold up a banner before a game that read 'Truth for Giulio Regeni,' the young Italian researcher killed in Egypt in circumstances that have never been clarified. And there was more ... On the poster advertising the team's summer training camp at Pinzolo – next to the caption 'The She-Wolf is coming back to the Dolomites' – was a close-up photo of one player, Mohamed Salah, celebrating a goal. Behind him, in the background, were Alessandro Florenzi, Daniele De Rossi and Totti, giving a Roman centurion salute. There was no doubt that Momo had won over his manager, club and the Roma public.

The Giallorossi's fans voted him player of the month for May, best new player and player of the season, ahead of Radja Nainggolan, Francesco Totti and Miralem Pjanić. The winner of the 2015–16 awards was described on the club website: 'Fast, powerful and a natural goal scorer, Salah's presence always causes big problems for opposition defences. He is a player who should not be given the slightest space [...] During the course of the season, he has showed off his complete repertoire, from his first goal against Sassuolo on the volley from outside the area, to the last, when he took AC Milan's defence apart at the San Siro. Despite the managerial change midway through the season, Salah has continued to delight the Roma fans, who are looking forward to seeing him again next season under the guidance of Luciano Spalletti, who has made him a key part of his attacking formation.' High praise indeed and a jackpot of awards. Not bad for a new arrival! Nevertheless, he was not entirely satisfied: 'I think it's been a good season, but we didn't win anything and that's a shame,' he answered when asked a question during his takeover of the club's official Twitter profile. He also shared that his aim for the coming season was to 'win a title with AS Roma to make our fans happy and to win the Africa Cup of Nations with Egypt'.

Chapter 13

Magical nights

'@22mosalah has completed a permanent transfer to Italian club Roma … Good luck Momo❤❤.'

Chelsea announced the Egyptian winger's move to the Giallorossi at 5.05pm on 3 August 2016. AS Roma had signed the player by paying the Blues the €15 million stipulated by the release clause established twelve months earlier. The news provoked an immediate reaction on social media: 'Honestly hope you're joking'; 'Don't know why they let him go'; 'Salah was better than Hazard last season'; 'Stupid choice'; 'Bad call, good for AS Roma.' For the most part, the reactions coming from fans of the London team were negative; they were convinced that it was only the Giallorossi who were getting something out of the deal. Without mincing words, they felt they had sold off one of the jewels in their crown for pocket money. Who did they hold responsible? This became an inevitable question when Salah later went on to triumph at Liverpool. 'My decision? No, no, no!' answered Antonio Conte, Chelsea manager when the permanent transfer was confirmed. 'I have never spoken about Salah because I think the situation was clear, very clear. No one asked me about him. No, I don't want to take this responsibility. If you put this on me, I'm in trouble. Put that on the person who has to take the responsibility.' This was an indirect swipe at José Mourinho, the manager who had allowed Salah to leave for Fiorentina in the first place. But the Special One was having none of it: 'Chelsea decided to sell him. And when they say that I was the one that sold him, it is a lie. I bought him. But he came as a young kid, physically he was not ready, mentally he was not ready, socially and culturally. He was lost and everything was tough for him. He wanted to play more minutes, to mature. He wanted to go and we sent him on loan. I thought it was necessary. But, after that, the decision to sell him and to use that money to buy another player wasn't mine.'

Controversies and truth aside, the news of his definitive transfer came while Mohamed Salah was right in the middle of a North American tour. The adventure had begun somewhat unexpectedly: Momo was turned back at the gate at Fiumicino Airport. He had not been able to fly to Boston with the team as his visa was deemed incomplete. The problem was resolved within a few days and the number 11 met up with his teammates at Harvard University's Ohiri Field for a training session. On 1 August, AS Roma took on Jürgen Klopp's Liverpool in St Louis. In the 62nd minute, a cross came in from an unmarked Florenzi for Džeko to head under the bar. Simon Mignolet parried the header from close range, but Salah came out of nowhere to slot in the Belgian keeper's attempted clearance. The final score was 2–1. Before returning to Italy, they played their second and last game against Didier Drogba's Montreal Impact on 3 August. It was to be the Romans' second victory. The 2–0 win came courtesy of a flat right-footed shot from Džeko and Radja Nainggolan, on the end of a penetrating assist from Salah. Roma's defence were unconvincing however and Alisson, their Brazilian keeper, was forced to work overtime.

These two American wins were a good omen with the Champions League play-off against Porto looming. In the first leg in the Estádio do Dragão on 17 August, Roma, reduced to ten men following the sending off of Thomas Vermaelen, held on to take a promising 1–1 draw back to the Italian capital. But the following week was a disaster and Roma conceded three goals, kissing goodbye to the Champions League after a game that the Giallorossi ended with only nine men, after both De Rossi and Emerson Palmieri received red cards. The club's fans were bitterly disappointed, but there was still the Europa League and Serie A, in which things were looking much better. On Saturday 15 October, with victory at the San Paolo against Maurizio Sarri's Napoli, Roma began to look like Juve's biggest rivals. Edin Džeko and Salah played key roles in the game. The Bosnian bomber scored twice, either side of half-time. After a goal from Koulibaly reignited Neapolitan hopes, Salah finished things off to make it 3–1. Roma were now in second, just five points behind top-of-the-table Juve. Džeko was Serie A's leading scorer with seven goals, while Momo had scored four, plus one in the Europa League against Astra Giurgiu. This did not count his assists for the Bosnian number 9, such as the one he provided after stealing the ball from Koulibaly for their first goal against Napoli.

Three weeks later and Momo was to have a magical night. At the Olimpico, against Bologna, in the late kick-off on the twelfth matchday of the season, in which he scored the first hat-trick of his career ... after almost missing the first goal. In the thirteenth minute, Perotti dummied a cross on the right that saw his yellow-shirted marker jump out of the way and allow him into the area to supply the cross. Near the penalty spot, Momo was off-balance and struck the ball poorly with his left foot. Adam Masina, the Bolognese full-back, lost the ball as Salah slid in to pick it up from Da Costa and turn it into the net. In the seventeenth minute of the second half,

Kevin Strootman picked up the ball in midfield and found a gap to put the number 11 through so all he had to do was beat the Brazilian keeper. And finally, in the 71st minute, on the edge of the Bolognese area, Salah released Džeko on the left but the Bosnian hit the post. Da Costa could not hold Momo back and the Egyptian stepped up to make it three. It could have been four or five if the number 11 had taken all his chances on that magical early November evening. But that was not all; there were also two assists to be counted – one for Perotti and another for Džeko – that had gone unrewarded. In keeping with tradition, the young Egyptian left with the ball under his arm after the final whistle. In the mixed zone, he said: 'I'm delighted about the hat-trick, but winning the game is the most important thing. I hope we can continue like this. We're four points behind Juve and we've now got the international break to recover. Then we'll have to play like we did today, win all our games and stay hot on the heels of the leaders.'

When Luciano Spalletti had recalled Mo to the bench in the 85th minute, he gave him a hug and a kiss; it was clear he had a soft spot for the unstoppable striker, but later, in the press conference, he crossed his t's and dotted his i's to make sure Mo did not rest on his laurels: 'Salah has to improve when we have possession. He often gets sucked into the defensive line. He either goes too quickly or waits too long, when he should play more of a part in the dribbling. If he can improve that as well, he'll be lethal.'

The following day's newspapers were not so gloomy: 'Salah, like a man possessed'; 'Outrageous Salah'; 'Salah, divine hat-trick'; 'Salah's magical night'; 'Salah the star'; 'Salah with a performance worthy of a standing ovation.' The praise was unanimous and it was followed by an analysis of the young man's development. He was no longer the player he had been in the previous season that had gone three months without scoring; he had scored eight times in the league. He was Roma's most prolific forward (seven on target at the Olimpico) and an assist-machine, gifting Džeko three goals since the start of the season. But despite the numbers and plaudits, the boy from Nagrig kept a low profile. He celebrated his teammates' goals but did not glorify his own with anything more than a simple glance upwards and a point to the skies in prayer.

'Salah is a great person. Very reserved, very respectful, humble and smiling. He's a player who loves his job and loves experiencing everything it gives him. He's a hard worker on the pitch, efficient, plays a key part in the team, is an asset upfront and a key player. Everyone appreciated him and he was loved by all. He was really recognised and applauded.' This is how he was described by Clément Grenier, the Olympique Lyonnais midfielder who arrived in Rome on loan during the winter transfer window.

'In the dressing room, Momo was next to Nainggolan and Totti. Close to Džeko, Manolas, De Rossi and Perotti, he got on with everyone even if he wasn't necessarily close to them. He was very kind, nice to everyone, from the directors to those lower down, and super discreet,' explains an insider at the club in the Italian capital. 'There was never anything written about his behaviour in the press.'

Momo was not a fan of partying or nightclubs. He lived with his wife Magi and Makka, his daughter, at Via Euripide, 123 in the Axa district, on an avenue shaded by umbrella pines, cypresses, palms and jasmine. He was rarely seen around the neighbourhood, even less so at the Le Terrazze shopping centre, often visited by other players. He preferred to stay in the quiet of his home, reading or playing with his two-and-a-half-year-old daughter. He would sometimes go

out for dinner with Stephan el-Shaarawy, the former Genoa
player with an Egyptian father who was helping him improve
his Italian. As often as he could, he would attend Friday
prayers at the Toba Mosque in Acilia, one of the most important Islamic centres in the Italian capital. 'The first time he
came on his own without warning. He turned up in his car
and parked outside,' remembers Ibrahim el-Robi, one of the
members of the community. 'He's a person with an impeccable character and vocation, demonstrating another quality
of the Islamic world that can't be found anywhere else. He's
unique. There have been other Muslim players in Rome but
he made the difference with his simplicity and kindness.'

'He didn't show off. He was humble. The whole community was proud of him,' explains eighteen-year-old Karim,
with a Roman accent.

'He was one of the faithful like any other. I spoke with him
once, one to one. A private conversation that lasted twenty
minutes, but I can't tell you about it. I can't tell you if we
talked about him leaving,' says the smiling Imam Mohamed
Afiz, who has been at the Toba Mosque for six years.

Momo Salah, a quiet man who turns into a man possessed
on the pitch, a player capable of inventing serpentine moves
and fatal incursions, built on a remarkable understanding
with Džeko. In early November, Europe's finest duo scored
eighteen goals, a tally no one could better. Not Messi-Suarez
(Barcelona), behind them with only sixteen, on a par with
Cavani-Lucas (PSG) and Diego Costa-Hazard (Chelsea).
Agüero-Sterling (Manchester City) were three off the pace,
with Cristiano Ronaldo-Bale (Real Madrid) even further
behind, with ten, not to mention Rooney-Ibrahimović
(Manchester United), with only seven. But unfortunately the
curse of the Rome derby lay just around the corner. In his
first season with the Giallorossi, Momo had been stretchered

off during the game against the Biancocelesti and this time he would not even make it onto the pitch. On 30 November, just before the game against Lazio, Vermaelen trod on his foot in the last few minutes of training, leaving him with a searing pain in his ankle. Salah left Trigoria on crutches and with an ice pack on the joint. Tests confirmed a lesion to the external ligament of his right ankle, affecting the anterolateral muscles and tendons. The doctors ruled him out of the upcoming games against Lazio, AC Milan, Juve and Chievo. Salah, busy with the Egyptian side in the Africa Cup of Nations from 17 January, would not be available to his manager until February. But his recovery was faster than expected and Salah returned to the pitch on 17 December in Turin. Coming on for the second half, he looked like a ghost of himself as the playmaker behind Džeko, and his bursts of speed were blocked at the outset, stopping him from bringing anything to fruition against Juventus. Thanks to a goal from Gonzalo Higuaín, the Bianconeri sealed their 25th consecutive home win in the league and topped the table after the first half of the season. The Old Lady had increased her lead with seven points over the Giallorossi. Roma's last game of the year came on 22 December, at home to Chievo. El-Shaarawy was the real Pharaoh that day: his free-kick provided Džeko with the ball to make it 2–1. Salah played 80 minutes before being replaced by Perotti, but he struggled and made too many silly mistakes. Roma won 3–1 and paid tribute to their Egyptian number 11. They knew just how much they were going to miss him.

Chapter 14

From Libreville to Liverpool

Three names were nominated for the Best Arab Player of the Year 2016: Medhi Benatia, Mohamed Salah and Riyad Mahrez. Gianni Infantino revealed the name of the winner at a gala dinner for the Dubai Globe Soccer Awards on 28 December. On stage at the Madinat Jumeirah Resort, the president of FIFA opened the envelope and announced: 'The winner is: Mohamed Salah.' A video of Mo's greatest goals in a Roma shirt began playing as he climbed onto the stage to receive the golden trophy to applause from the audience. Holding the microphone, dressed in a dark suit and white shirt, Momo answered in English as the presenter asked him a question about his biggest moments: in 2016, he had scored eighteen goals for Roma and five for the national side. An emotional Salah confirmed, with a dry mouth: 'Yes, of course, so far this is the best moment for me. I scored many goals for the club and many goals for the national team.'

'Talking about the national team: two games, two victories you are already on your way to Russia for the World Cup?' the presenter asked. 'Yes, we have six points now. I think we are doing well but we still have a long way,' replied Salah. 'I hope we can win and we have to qualify for the World Cup. For us it's like a dream. We have to work hard for this. Let's see ...'

Things may have already been looking good for the World

Cup, but before that there was the Africa Cup of Nations. The Pharaohs had been absent since 2010, when they won the trophy for the third consecutive time. After crashing out during qualifying in 2012 and 2015, the anticipation in Egypt to see the team now managed by the Argentine Héctor Cúper was huge. There was also plenty of attention from the Italian press, thanks to the presence of the Roma striker. The bookmakers named Egypt among the favourites for the title, but things did not get off to a good start. The Pharaohs could only manage a goalless draw in their opening game against Mali in Gabon's Port-Gentil on 17 January. The team were flat and Salah was disappointing, substituted in the 69th minute after receiving a caution for a nasty tackle on Yacouba Sylla. In their second match, Egypt faced Uganda, who were bottom of Group D. A draw or a defeat would leave the Pharaohs in danger of being sent home much earlier than expected. On paper, it seemed like an easy game, but instead it took 88 minutes before the team managed by the former Inter manager could break the deadlock. Salah pulled off a great move in the box: he drew three defenders to him, dummied a shot and instead passed it to el-Said, who ran up to fire the ball with his right foot under the legs of Denis Onyango, the Ugandan number 1. This time the red-shirted number 10 did not disappoint. Assists apart, he had created two of the most promising chances for his team: in the 24th minute, a lob that just missed the goal and a one-on-one with Onyango that the keeper won.

Momo was also decisive in the final group game against a Ghanaian team that had already qualified. In the eleventh minute, he unleashed a powerful free-kick with the outside of his left foot that flew over the wall and into the top corner. There was nothing Brimah Razak could do. The 1–0 result saw Egypt through to the quarter-finals as group winners. On

29 January, they played a Morocco team coached by Hervé Renard, the French manager who had won two Africa Cup of Nations – in 2012 with Zambia and in 2015 with Ivory Coast. The pitch was barely playable. Egypt got off to a better start, but the Atlas Lions racked up crosses and chances in the second half. The closest came when Mbark Boussoufa hit the crossbar in the 55th minute. The Pharaohs held on and with less than two minutes to go to extra time, substitute Mahmoud Kahraba finally found the winning strike. A cross from the left-hand corner flag sent the ball bobbling around in front of the goal as Kahraba beat Medhi Benatia, the Moroccan captain, to it and half bicycle-kicked it into the goal to send Egypt into the semi-final.

Against Burkina Faso on 1 February, the national hero was el-Hadary, Egypt's green-shirted 44-year-old goalkeeper. During the penalty shootout, the veteran keeper, with four AFCON titles already behind him, saved the fourth kick from his young opposite number Hervé Koffi and the final penalty taken by Bertrand Traoré. The Egyptians went crazy as the Stallions despaired. They had dominated the game and played better than their rivals, but failed to land the knock-out blow. With the score line at 1–1 after 120 minutes it all came down to the penalty spot. Mohamed Salah had scored the goal that gave Egypt the short-lived lead in the 66th minute: after Kahraba laid the ball off to him, he wasted no time half-volleying it with his left foot for his fourth shot from the edge of the area. Later on, he was the first to embrace el-Hadary. Egypt had reached their ninth final and harboured dreams of bringing home their eighth title.

The final act of the African Cup of Nations was played out in the Stade de l'Amitié in Libreville on 5 February. Hugo Broos's Cameroon stood in the Pharaohs' way. To get this far, the Indomitables Lions had beaten both Senegal and

Ghana, two of the tournament favourites, in the quarter-final and semi-final respectively. It had been a fairy tale for them: a Belgian manager who had been appointed after seeing the job advertised on the Cameroon federation's website, a national side that had to do without eight of its most experienced players who had refused their call-ups to stay in Europe, and a team that had been forced to find its heroes well behind the front lines. In the final match of the group stage, Fabrice Ondoa, who hardly ever got time on the pitch for the Sevilla B team, pulled off a fantastic stop in the dying moments of the game to knock out the hosts Gabon. Even in the final, these unlikely heroes upset the form books. Mohamed Elneny, the Arsenal midfielder, supplied by his friend and former teammate Mohamed Salah, surprised Ondoa with a violent right-footed shot inside the near post to give the Pharaohs the lead in the 21st minute.

With the scoreboard in their favour, Cúper's men stepped off the gas, convinced they could protect their narrow 1–0 lead. And protect it they did in the first half, but after the break, the Lions' attacking runs and bursts of speed from the Danish club Aalborg's Christian Bassogog became increasingly dangerous. Then Nicolas Nkoulou, who was standing in as central defender for the injured Teikeu, soared with an imperious header to score the equaliser. It came as a blow to the team in red, who struggled to react. Their only weapon came in the form of long balls in search of the fast-footed Salah, who came up with one of his sudden stops and back-heels to almost change the face of the game. But it was not to be; in the 88th minute, Vincent Aboubakar, the number 10, the Beşiktaş striker, the man whom Broos had thrown into the fray in the second half to replace Ndip Tambe, delivered a stunning piece of skill. He controlled the ball with his chest on the edge of the area, sombrero flicked it over his opponent's head and, before it could fall back to earth, half-volleyed it with his right foot past a stunned el-Hadary. The Cameroonian fans began partying in the stands. Roger Milla and Samuel Eto'o celebrated in the VIP box. After a fifteen-year wait, Cameroon had won their fifth continental title and got their revenge for the defeat inflicted by the Pharaohs nine years earlier.

There would be nothing for Egypt but great sadness. For Héctor Cúper it was his fifth lost final, from the Champions League to the Copa del Rey and the Cup Winners' Cup. In total, he had seen seven titles vanish from his grasp. For him and for Egypt, there was nothing left to do but mourn and focus on qualifying for the Russia World Cup, an objective they had not achieved since Italia 90. For Salah, before his next commitments with the national side came four months of matches with Roma, who posted the following on their website after the tournament in Africa: 'Congratulations Momo! We're still proud of you!'

Two days after the final, Momo was on the bench at the Olimpico; he did not play but instead watched the Giallorossi overwhelm his former club 4–0. He returned to the pitch for 80 minutes at Crotone in the 24th Serie A game of the season but failed to score; he eventually rediscovered the back of the net the following week against Torino. Despite beating Olympique Lyonnais at home on 16 March, Roma were out of the Europa League. The first leg counted in these last sixteen knock-out games and the Giallorossi had been beaten 4–2 in France. History repeated itself on 4 April. At home, Spalletti's men beat their eternal cross-city rivals Lazio 3–2, with two goals courtesy of Momo and one from el-Shaarawy, but in the return derby Lazio triumphed 2–0. The second title of the season then went up in smoke. On 28 May 2017, the 38th and final matchday of the Serie A season, Roma finished second, four points behind Juventus, Italian champions for the sixth successive time. Edin Džeko, the Bosnian, was the league's top scorer with 29 goals. He had the service he received from Salah to thank, as the Egyptian had devoted plenty to supplying him with stunning assists just waiting to be finished off. The Giallorossi's number 11 had provided the most assists in Serie A, with ten, just behind José María Callejón, with twelve, but Callejón had played seven more matches than the Egyptian. Momo had made 31 appearances in Serie A and scored fifteen goals; he had made six appearances and scored two goals in both the Europa League and the Coppa Italia. Once again, the number 11's desire for a title would go unfulfilled. He had gone yet another season without winning anything with the Giallorossi. And it was to be his last.

Three days after the end of the English league season, the news came that Mohammed Salah was one step away from signing for Liverpool. On 3 June, the Italian press wrote that the Reds had convinced the Egyptian about his footballing future at the club and offered him a four-year €5.5 million contract, including bonuses. Ramy Abbas, Mo's agent, flew to London to clarify the terms of the agreement and turned the Liverpool offer over to Roma: €35 million. At Trigoria they wanted at least €50 or €55 million, a figure the English club did not seem willing to consider. But the negotiations continued. Ramón Rodríguez Verdejo 'Monchi', the director of football recently arrived from Sevilla, was keen to point out that Roma was 'not a supermarket. There has been interest in Salah, but the price will be set by Roma, not the buyers.'

Mo had seemingly made the decision to return to the Premier League sometime earlier and had met with some Liverpool intermediaries in a restaurant in central Rome back in March. According to insiders, the dinner ended with a toast to his new adventure in England. He was now impatient for the negotiations to conclude quickly so he could begin the long bureaucratic process of obtaining a residency permit. Unlike the story of his move to Roma, this time it did not drag on.

On 22 June, Liverpool Football Club announced with a statement released on social media that it had completed 'the signing of Mohamed Salah from Roma. The 25 year old agreed a long-term contract with the Reds on Thursday after completing a medical. He will officially become an LFC player on July 1, 2017.'

AS Roma confirmed: 'The Egyptian footballer will move to the English club for a fixed price of €42 million, and variable, up to a maximum of €8 million, for bonuses linked to the achievement of certain sporting objectives by the English club and the player.'

Sometime later Monchi would explain: 'We had to sell him by 30 June to comply with UEFA Financial Fair Play regulations. We had no other solutions: he wanted to leave and we were forced to sell him.'

Basel's Joo Ho Park fights for the ball against Salah during a friendly match between Switzerland's FC Basel and Egypt's Olympic Team at the Rankhof Stadium on 16 March 2012. The Basel club president watched the match, seeing Salah score two of the four Egyptian goals, confirming his decision to sign him.

Georgios Kefalas/EPA/Shutterstock

(below) Salah celebrates his first goal for Chelsea on 22 March 2016, in a 6–0 win against Arsenal.
Andy Rain/EPA/Shutterstock

Playing for Roma, Salah scores his first hat-trick on 6 November 2016 against Bologna in Serie A at the Olimpico Stadium.
Claudio Peri/EPA/Shutterstock

In his first Champions League match with Liverpool, Salah scores against Watford on 12 August 2017 to make the score 3–2. The game ends 4–2 and Salah is finally able to make his mark on a competition that he loves.
Peter Powell/EPA-EFE/Shutterstock

above) Celebrating with his Egyptian teammates after winning the 2018 FIFA World Cup Qualifier match against Congo at Borg El-Arab Stadium, Alexandria, Egypt on 8 October 2017. Salah scores both goals in the 2–1 win.
PA Images/Shutterstock

26 May 2018, Champions League Final match against Real Madrid, a devastated Salah is injured, dislocating his shoulder, and has to be substituted. He leaves the stadium for the hospital, not watching his team lose 1–3.
Kieran Mcmanus/BPI/Shutterstock

At the Liverpool Awards Dinner in Anfield, on 10 May 2018, Salah wins two awards – Player's Player of the Season and Overall Player of the Season. Later that night he flies to London, to receive football's oldest individual accolade, the Football Writers' Association Footballer of the Year.
Andrew Powell/Liverpool FC via Getty Images

Salah is all smiles as Liverpool are crowned champions of England for the first time in 30 years. Anfield, 22 July 2020.
Magi Haroun/Shutterstock

Chapter 15

A pacey winger

Jürgen Klopp was happy. Salah had been one of his transfer window targets to strengthen the Liverpool squad ahead of the Champions and Premier leagues and the club had responded accordingly. On the official website, the German manager welcomed Salah and his family with the following statement, which smacked not of a cliché but of real esteem: 'Mohamed has the perfect mix of experience and potential – this is a really exciting signing for us. He knows the Premier League,' Klopp explained. 'He has pedigree in the Champions League and he is one of the most important players for his country. His record in Italy has been outstanding and he possesses qualities that will enhance our team and squad. I have followed him since he emerged at Basel and he has matured into a really good player. His pace is incredible, he gives us more attacking threat and we are already strong in this area. I like that we will make it even more competitive. Most important though, for us, is that he is hungry, willing and eager to be even better and improve further. He believes in what we are trying to do here at Liverpool and is extremely keen to be part of it. He is very excited about performing for our wonderful supporters. He is an ambitious player who wants to win and win at the highest level; he knows he can fulfil those ambitions with Liverpool.'

Mohamed Salah, who had just arrived in the city, with the ink still wet on his new contract, answered on

Liverpoolfc.com: 'I'm very excited to start the season with Klopp. Everyone knows he is a great man and a great coach. Everyone can see he gives everything. I will give 100 per cent for the club. We have a great team and very good players. I was watching the games last year and everyone was giving 100 per cent. I hope to see that together we can win something for the club, for the supporters and for us.'

Klopp and Salah had a great mutual respect and were on the same wavelength. Giving 100 per cent for the team was the basis of the German coach's philosophy. Klopp and Salah held each other in high esteem and had common goals. Mohamed Salah was keen to demonstrate that his time at Chelsea had been nothing but an unfortunate interlude, that everything was different now and he would be able to show off his football to the full. He was four years older, more mature and had gained experience at Fiorentina and Roma; on paper, he now had everything he needed to impose himself in the Premier League. Jürgen Klopp saw great potential in the 25-year-old Egyptian and hoped he would bring even more quality to his strike force.

But not even the German manager could have imagined what the Reds' number 11 would pull off in the 2017–18 season. Nor did Salah himself, the fans in the Kop or the club's directors. Many looked on the new arrival with scepticism. More than anything because of the figure Liverpool had forked out: a record transfer that had exceeded the £35 million paid by Kenny Dalglish to Newcastle for Andy Carroll in 2011. Back in 2013, Brendan Rodgers had seen the player pinched from under his nose by Chelsea when he could have bought him for less than £15 million. Regrets aside, despite Salah's 300 appearances in league games and international cups, despite the 34 goals he had scored in two seasons with the Giallorossi, there were doubts about what Mo could bring to Liverpool. Yes, of course, he was a pacey winger with impeccable dribbling skills, but for many fans he was not a big enough name. He might have been good back-up for Sadio Mané, but definitely not a goal machine like Luis Suárez or Fernando Torres, to name only two foreign players who had gone on the rampage at Anfield. To prove the naysayers wrong, Salah started like a rocket.

Momo made his debut in the red number 11 shirt during the second pre-season friendly against Wigan Athletic at the DW Stadium on 14 July, and scored his first goal. Philippe Coutinho stole the ball in midfield for a pass to Roberto Firmino. The number 9 continued into the box and gifted an exquisite pass to Salah, who knew the keeper would come off his line and scored to make it 1–1. It was the end of the first half and the newcomer had given a glimpse of his repertoire as early as the 60th second of the game when, speeding away from everyone down the right wing, his cross flew just over the crossbar.

The pre-season warm-ups continued and Momo kept on scoring. He found the net against Leicester in the final of the Premier League Asia Trophy in Hong Kong on 22 July. It was his first trophy with Liverpool. On 29 July, Hertha Berlin and Liverpool marked the 125th anniversary of their foundation with a gala game at the Olympic Stadium in the German capital. Salah celebrated his third goal to seal the Reds' 3–0 win. He also scored the second in the semi-final of the Audi Cup against Bayern Munich on 1 August.

Summer tournaments and friendlies were one thing, but Momo continued to make his presence felt when the Premier League season started. The first game of the season saw Liverpool away at Watford on 12 August. Salah was in the starting line-up in a three-pronged attack alongside Mané and Firmino, the trio who would go on to stun Europe with their understanding as the season went on.

The number 19, number 9 and number 11 would all score that day. Sadio Mané got the first to make it 1–1. Thanks to a clumsy foul by Gomes, the Watford goalkeeper, Salah then won a penalty; Roberto Firmino made no mistake with the conversion. Two minutes later, the Brazilian returned the favour for Momo with a stunning lob that sailed over the defence as the new number 11 was one step ahead in finding the back of the net. He spread his arms wide and ran to the stands with his tongue out like Michael Jordan of old and punched the air before hugging Firmino. On the bench, Klopp beat his chest like a modern-day Tarzan. The game ended 3–3: a goal conceded in the 93rd minute thanks to a howler of a defensive error from Liverpool spoiled the party. The German manager was furious because, not only had Miguel Britos equalised from an offside position, but his defence had conceded two sloppy goals. Firmino was man of the match, but the new signing had 'shown what he can do for us,' according to Klopp. It was a great return to the Premier League ... it was as if an age had passed since 1 January 2015, when Momo had made his last appearance in a Blues shirt in Chelsea's 5–3 loss to Tottenham.

The time had also come for Salah to make his mark on the score sheet in a competition he loved so much: the Champions League. Twenty-third of August saw the return leg of the play-offs for the biggest competition in continental club football: Liverpool faced the German team TSG 1899 Hoffenheim at home. The away leg had finished 2–1 to the Reds, which augured well for the rematch. But Klopp is not given to speculation. The best form of defence is attack and Liverpool embodied this philosophy in front of their home fans from the kick-off. In twenty chaotic minutes, they scored three goals, although it could have been four or five. Salah bagged the second. Firmino ran into the box from the left before crossing to a waiting Georginio Wijnaldum, who clattered the ball against the right post, but Momo was there to pick up the rebound and knock it in. The game ended 4–2.

'It has been a brilliant night,' said Jordan Henderson, the captain. 'The atmosphere was brilliant, we were brilliant at the start and set the tempo. We let in a couple of goals so we have still got things to work on but overall we're delighted to get back into the Champions League where Liverpool belong.' The Reds had been absent from European football's elites since the 2014–15 season and their return delighted the club's fans. But the fun had only just started. Four days later, the team posted another very satisfying win, thrashing Arsène Wenger's Arsenal 4–0. Petr Čech denied Salah twice. The keeper in his trademark black head guard pulled off some astonishing saves and there was nothing the Egyptian could do. When he did eventually score, the goal was disallowed as the assistant referee had already raised his flag for offside. But so much goal-mouth action ultimately drew its just rewards. The move began from an Arsenal corner cleared by the Reds' defence. Salah picked up the ball, sprinted 60 yards and outfoxed Čech with a low shot that grazed the post and ended up in the back of the net. There was more to come … in the 77th minute, Mo conjured up a perfect cross for a running Sturridge to fire past the Gunners' keeper to finish off the game.

As pointed out by the English press, Momo had scored more goals (three) since the beginning of the season with Liverpool than in two years at Chelsea (two). And in less than a month since he had first pulled on the red number 11 shirt, he had scored seven times. Although the media spotlight was on Sadio Mané, seen as a possible successor to Luis

Suárez, Klopp and the Kop were beginning to realise that the Egyptian was more than just a pacey winger and could make his own contribution to the spoils bagged by Mané and Firmino.

The Premier League took a break for the 2018 Russia World Cup qualifiers. Egypt had two games coming up, both against Uganda. The Pharaohs were beaten 1–0 at the Mandela National Stadium in Kampala on 31 August and lost the lead in Group E, but five days later, Mo Salah helped them get their revenge in Alexandria. He found himself on his own in front of Denis Onyango on the end of an exquisite ball from Elneny in the fifth minute. The yellow-shirted keeper stopped the shot but could not hold on to the ball and Mo turned it in. With nine points, the Pharaohs returned to the top of their group, while Uganda were in second with seven points, Ghana in third with five and Congo bottom of the table with one point and no chance of qualifying. Les Diables Rouges would be Salah and Co.'s next opponents in the penultimate African qualifying game.

After success with the national side came a beating inflicted by Manchester City. On 9 September, Pep Guardiola's men overwhelmed Liverpool, down to ten men after Mané's red card. It was the first defeat of the season for Klopp and a clear message from the Citizens to any potential rivals: the Premier League is ours this year. Things improved slightly on 13 September in the first Champions League group game. At Anfield, the Reds played host to Sevilla, the team that had beaten them 3–1 in the Europa League final on 18 May 2016. The Spanish team immediately took the lead through Ben Yedder, who exploited an error from Dejan Lovren in the fifth minute to make it 1–0. Liverpool reacted: a low cross came in from the left courtesy of Alberto Moreno for Firmino to tap in and level things up in the twentieth minute. Salah took care of giving his team the lead. He stubbornly nabbed the ball from the feet of Steven Nzonzi just outside the area. The Frenchman ended up on the ground but the referee saw nothing amiss. Momo did not need to be asked twice and shot with his left. Taking a deflection off a defender, the ball wrong-footed Sergio Rico. It seemed as if Liverpool's first Champions League game in three years was going to end with the best possible result but then Joaquín Correa, the Argentine midfielder, equalised to make it 2–2 in the 72nd minute. Once again, defensive fragility had cost the Reds dearly. 'We know we have to improve,' said Klopp, after the game. 'But there is so much potential and we can work with this. It is a draw – it does not feel too good but I am fine with big parts of the performance.'

Mohamed Salah scored two more goals in the next three league games. He equalised to seal a home draw against Burnley then opened the scoring in the away win against Leicester on 23 September. But he failed to score away at Newcastle on 1 October against a Magpies team managed by the former Liverpool boss Rafa Benítez.

This was followed by another international break: Mohamed Salah flew to Alexandria to play the fifth and penultimate African World Cup qualifier. Top of Group E, Egypt faced Congo, who were languishing at the bottom. Three wins and a loss for the North Africans (five goals scored and two conceded), compared with one draw and three losses for Congo, the only team still yet to win a group game. They had conceded nine goals (the worst defence in the group) and only scored three themselves. On paper, it looked like an easy win for Egypt ... but in football, as in life, nothing should ever be taken for granted.

Chapter 16

The 94th minute

'Alexandria. At last. Alexandria. Lady of the Dew. Bloom of white nimbus. Bosom of radiance, wet with sky water. Core of nostalgia steeped in honey and tears.' This was how Naguib Mahfouz, winner of the Nobel Prize for Literature in 1988, described the city on the Mediterranean in the opening to *Miramar*. The city founded by Alexander the Great, the cradle of Hellenistic culture, home to both the greatest library in Antiquity and the famous lighthouse, one of the Seven Wonders of the World, and the place where Erastosthenes of Cyrene calculated the terrestrial meridian. Alexandria, the cosmopolitan metropolis, capital of Egypt for 600 years, backdrop to the stories of Cleopatra and Marcus Aurelius, Octavian and Ptolemy, Napoleon and Muhammad Ali Pasha, Laurence Durrell's Alexandria Quartet and the British secret service. Cairo may well be the seat of military power, the nerve centre and economic hub of the country, but Alexandria is historically synonymous with culture, as well as a hotbed for political and new social movements. It gave birth to the 'silent uprising', the first protest against the atrocities of the Hosni Mubarak regime. These silent demonstrations were organised via Facebook after 28-year-old Khaled Mohamed Saeed was killed by the security forces on 6 June 2010. His swollen face and the Kullum Khaled Saeed group (We are all Khaled Saeed) became the banner under which an unprecedented mobilisation and the seed of the Egyptian spring rallied.

Here in Alexandria, where football is a passion, as it is all over the country, Egypt took on Congo in the Borg el-Arab stadium on 8 October 2017. It was a game that could see the Pharaohs qualify for a World Cup, their first in 28 years. Twenty-eight years earlier, what would go down in history as the 'hate match' was played against Algeria in Cairo on 17 November 1989. The first leg had ended in a goalless draw and it all came down to the game at the International Stadium in front of a 100,000-strong crowd. In the fourth minute, Hossam Hassan scored the headed goal that sent Egypt to Italia 90. A riot broke out after the final whistle. The Algerians surrounded the match officials, the opposing players and even attacked the VIP area. An Egyptian team doctor was hit by a bottle and blinded in one eye. The finger was pointed at Lakhdar Belloumi, the Algerian star and African Footballer of the Year in 1981. He denied all responsibility and eyewitnesses claimed the act had instead been perpetrated by Kamel Kadri, keeper for Les Fennecs. Despite this, Belloumi was convicted in absentia and an international arrest warrant was issued and not rescinded until twenty years later.

Egypt failed to get beyond the group stage at Italia 90. They finished bottom of Group F after two draws with Ireland and Holland and defeat to England. They scored a single goal, from the penalty spot, courtesy of Magdi Abdelghani, in the 1–1 draw with Holland.

Twenty years later, footballing war between Egypt and Algeria broke out once again during qualifying for the 2010 World Cup. At the end of qualification, the Pharaohs and Les Fennecs were level on points won, goals scored and goals conceded. They had to play-off at a neutral venue for the right to fly to South Africa. The deciding game was played on 18 November 2009 in Khartoum, or rather in Omdurman, the Sudanese capital's twin city on the opposite bank of the Nile. The atmosphere was extremely tense given what had happened in Cairo four days earlier, during what should have been the final qualifying game: the Algerian team bus had been stoned by Egyptian fans and three players were injured before even setting foot on the pitch. After the goal from Emad Moteab in the 96th minute made it 2–0, bringing the Pharaohs back in to it and leaving the Greens needing a draw, all hell had broken loose. There were clashes both inside and outside the stadium. The headquarters of Egypt Air and the branch of the Egyptian company Orascom in Algiers were attacked and violent scuffles between the two North African communities in Paris and Marseille followed. The press and television channels in the two countries did nothing but add fuel to the fire.

Four days later Khartoum was in a state of siege, with schools and public offices closed, the number of tickets reduced from 45,000 to 30,000 and 15,000 police officers deployed to prevent incidents between the opposing fans. In the end, everything went smoothly in the stadium; this time there was no declaration of war. Thanks to a goal from Antar Yahia in the 40th minute, Algeria qualified for the final stages of a World Cup for the third time. Yet again, Egypt were left empty-handed. The Egyptian federation could do nothing but ask FIFA to open an investigation into the Algerian delegation, claiming that the lives of fans, players and technical staff had been put at risk before and after the match. The investigation would ultimately conclude with the EFA instead receiving a punishment for lax security measures during the match played in Cairo!

Another blow came four years later. Egypt were thrashed 6–1 by Ghana's Black Stars in Kumasi. There was to be no miracle during the return leg in Cairo: on 19 November 2013

– in Aboutrika's last game for his national side in a number 22 shirt – the Pharaohs won 2–1 but Ghana's Muntari, Essien, Asamoah and Prince-Boateng boarded the plane the following summer for Brazil.

A certain imaginative right-winger, then at Basel, was on the pitch for both games: Mohamed Salah. He was a twenty-year-old who, four years later, would get his revenge in Alexandria on 8 October 2017 …

In the 62nd minute, Egypt picked up the ball in the midfield as it found its way to Elneny. The guy with the big head and beard in the number 17 shirt chipped the ball towards the box from the right touchline. It took a deflection off a Congolese defender's head, prolonging its trajectory and leaving one of his teammates stranded. With the ball still in the air, Mohamed Salah watched it, following its flight, controlling it with his right foot and knocking it on. For a moment, it seemed as if it would get away from him. But the number 10 managed to reach it with the toe of his left foot and got the better of the advancing Congolese goalkeeper to make it 1–0. Mo sped off towards the stands, pursued by his teammates. He ripped off his shirt and was overwhelmed by a seemingly never-ending hug. Substitutes, technical staff and a handful of fans invaded the pitch. There was little more than half an hour to go. The Pharaohs' veteran keeper Essam el-Hadary went crazy. Tinged with red, covered in Egyptian flags and submerged by the sound of vuvuzelas – reminiscent of the African World Cup – the stadium was like a volcano about to erupt. Medhat Shalabi, the match commentator, just kept screaming Salah's name and giving thanks to Allah. The only one who seemed to remain more or less calm was Héctor Cúper. Before the game, 'El Hombre Vertical' had had to take something to help him cope with the pressure. Staying calm was definitely the best option!

It took more than two minutes for the game to restart, before Salah, pointing his fingers to the skies, returned to the pitch, leaving the lights of thousands and thousands of phones twinkling in the stands, capturing the moment.

But in the 87th minute, Arnold Bouka Moutou – aged 28, born in Reims, the left-back who played for Dijon in France's Ligue 1 – silenced the Borg el-Arab stadium. Running up from midfield, he strained to get to the ball as a pinpoint cross came in; apparently forgotten by the Egyptian defenders, he volleyed the ball with his powerful left foot, leaving the green-shirted keeper with no chance. Fans in the stands cried, screamed, swore and held their heads in their hands as the commentator continued chanting like a lullaby '*Maaleish, maaleish, maaleish, maaleish*', (It's OK, it's OK, it's OK). Mo Salah was in the midfield, away from the action. When the ball hit the back of the net, he took his curls in his hands and collapsed onto the turf. By the look of him, it seemed to be all over. That's what everyone in the stadium thought. The Liverpool winger remained motionless, kicking the ground. Then, slowly, he came up onto his knees, raised his palms to the sky, stood up, picked up the ball and threw it away forcefully. He then brought his hands up to his face, desperate and exhausted, wearing a tragic expression. He clapped and shouted towards his teammates to raise their spirits and lifted up his arms to encourage the fans to support their team in the dying moments of the game.

In the 93rd minute, a cross came into the Congolese box. Mahmoud Hassan, known by the nickname Trezeguet, stopped the ball on his chest but it reared up again as Fernand Mayembo tried to take control before falling onto the Egyptian striker who made his third penalty appeal in two minutes. The action continued as the ball flew up high into the air just outside the away team's box. The recent substitute Merveil Ndockyt failed to control it and it fell at the feet of Ahmed Hegazy, the West Bromwich Albion central defender. The 26 year old turned and fed the ball into the box. Bodies were suddenly on the ground near the penalty spot. Trying to get ahead of Trezeguet, Beranger Itoua had brought him down. This time it was a penalty! Medhat Shalabi shouted 'Allah Akbar!' as many as seven times while the players, staff and fans jumped up and down before kneeling to thank Allah or divine providence. No one on the pitch, in the stands or in the television booth seemed to remember that penalties still have to be converted ...

In the 94th minute, Mohamed Salah held the ball in his hands. It seemed as if he said something to it before pressing it to his forehead and placing it on the spot. He banished the memory of the previous day's training when Essam el-Hadary had saved three of his penalties. He took a few paces back and kissed the shield on his shirt, as a Congolese defender finally left the area and spat at the ball. Salah passed his tongue over his lips, looked around him and started on his short run-up. Kicking the ball with his left foot, he put all the strength he had in his body into it. The goalkeeper went one way, the ball went the other: 2–1! Egypt had qualified for the 2018 Russia World Cup! The pitch was invaded, Salah was lifted up in triumph and celebrations broke out in the stands, in the streets and all over Egypt. It lasted until dawn. The commentator started crying and could only manage to say: 'Our country, our beloved Egypt.' Inas Mazhar, the stadium announcer, remained silent. She had no more words. 'Tears were rolling from the eyes of everyone: the players, the staff on the bench, the security officers,' she later told CNN. 'This means so much for Egypt. We are making history.' And there was no doubt that the hero of this chapter in Egypt's history was Mohamed Salah. A fortnight after the game,

Mamdouh Abbas, the businessman and former president of Zamalek (who had once opted not to take Salah because he thought he was not ready), offered Momo a luxury villa as a gift in gratitude for his role in the World Cup qualification. The Egyptian number 10 kindly thanked him but said that instead of giving him a villa a donation to his village of Nagrig would make him happy. A *beau geste* that won over everyone in Egypt, even the few non-football fans.

Chapter 17

Living a dream

It was snowing in Liverpool. White flakes floated down onto Anfield. At 2.15pm on 10 December, Craig Pawson blew the whistle to signal the start of the 229th Merseyside derby. Jürgen Klopp left Philippe Coutinho and Roberto Firmino on the bench. After a mid-week Champions League game (a 7–0 thrashing of Spartak Moscow), the manager had chosen to employ a rotation system. A decision he would come to regret. Sam Allardyce, the Everton boss, had opted for a 4-1-4-1 formation: defending to the bitter end to contain the Reds' attacking runs while providing long balls for Dominic Calvert-Lewin and Oumar Niasse. From the outset, Liverpool dominated to such an extent that by the end of the game they would have 79 per cent possession. But the siege they were laying to the Toffees' goal was proving fruitless. The cold Sunday afternoon was gloomy for the fans in the Kop, at least until Salah lit up the pitch at 2.58pm, 42 minutes into the first half. Liverpool were awarded a free-kick in Everton's midfield for a foul by Idrissa Gueye on Mané. The ball travelled from the left into the centre and then as far as Joe Gomez on the right wing. The defender with Gambian heritage spotted Mo on the edge of the opposition's box. The number 11 freed himself from the grip of Cuco Martina, jumped over Gueye and struck the ball with his left foot. It span around the blue number 5 Ashley Williams and ended up in the far top corner. Jordan Pickford was powerless to stop it.

Salah slid across the turf on his knees with his arms wide before his teammates arrived to hug him. After the game, Klopp was incensed with the referee, who had later awarded Everton a penalty, allowing Wayne Rooney to even things up. He was furious because he had seen three points go up in smoke thanks to a mistake by his defence, but there was no doubt that Mo's goal had been 'a wonderful strike'. It was the Egyptian's thirteenth Premier League goal; he had already scored four more than the entire Swansea City team! His record showed nineteen goals in 24 appearances in a Reds shirt.

Almost a year later, on 24 September 2018, that goal against his club's eternal rivals Everton would earn Salah the FIFA Puskás Award for the goal of the 2017–18 season. He beat Cristiano Ronaldo and his incredible bicycle kick against Juventus in the Champions League, and Gareth Bale, who pulled off the same technique in the final in Kiev. This was somewhat surprising given the sheer beauty of both the Portuguese and Welsh players' strikes, but the winner of the Puskás Award is chosen by online votes and Salah has millions and millions of fans. Talking of awards … on 11 December 2017, the day after his wonder goal in the derby, the BBC awarded him the title of African Footballer of the Year for 2017. Fans had overwhelmed the BBC.com/Africanfootball website with their votes. Mo beat Pierre-Emerick Aubameyang, Naby Keita, Sadio Mané and Victor Moses. He was the third Egyptian player – after Mohamed Barakat (2005) and Mohamed Aboutrika (2008) – to win the accolade. Riyad Mahrez, the Manchester City winger then with Leicester, had won it the year before. 'I am very happy to win this award,' said Momo. 'It's always a special feeling when you win something. You feel like you did a great year, so I'm very happy. I would also like to win

it next year.' For now he would have to 'content' himself
with having his title confirmed in Accra, Ghana on 4 January
2018. The captains, coaches and managers of Africa's teams
awarded him the CAF African Player of the Year for 2017 title
ahead of his teammate Mané and Aubameyang. 'Winning
this award is a dream come true. I think this title is helping
me a lot. I want to win it for a second time, for a third time,
for a fourth time. If I can win it twenty times I would be
happy,' said Salah, after receiving the award. He dedicated it
'to the kids in Egypt and Africa. I want to tell them to never
stop dreaming.'

Egypt hit the jackpot in Accra: the Pharaohs were named
best team and Héctor Cúper the best manager on the African
continent. This recognition was the result of reaching the
AFCON final and qualification for their first World Cup in
28 years. Thanks to Salah's impressive start to the season
with Liverpool, the distinctions were mounting up: two days
before the ceremony in Accra, he was also recognised as
the Arab Player of the Year for 2017, voted for by a hundred
sports journalists, and, on 1 January, saw nine pages dedicated to him by *Al Watan* with the title 'The Pharaoh: Joy of
2017 and Hope of 2018.'

So much good news but also some bad. On 6 January, the
Fab Four became three. Philippe Coutinho, the Brazilian,
who had already been on the point of leaving during the
summer, departed for Barcelona for a fee understood to be
£146 million, the most expensive signing in the history of
the Catalan club. Kevin Murphy from Cork, a Reds super-
fan, composed the following for Klopp to the tune of the
1969 song 'Sugar, Sugar' by The Archies: 'Salah, Mané, Mané
and Bobby Firmino but we sold Coutinho, but we got Salah!
Mané do do do do do!' The song and its chorus really caught
on.

In the meantime, the German manager was forced to explain that he and the club had done everything they could to hold on to the Brazilian and consequently he had been left with no choice – selling him had been an 'easy' decision. Klopp would now have to content himself with the Fab Three, but claimed that whenever a dominant character leaves a team, someone has to step up and fill the gap. And that person was to be Mohamed Salah.

By 13 February, just before the first knock-out stage of the Champions League against Porto, the number 11 had 21 league and one FA Cup goals behind him. Unfortunately, Liverpool had gone out of the cup after losing to West Bromwich Albion in the fourth round. In an interview with *FourFourTwo*, a laughing Mo said: 'I don't want to sound arrogant but, yeah! I expected to score a lot of goals. I was comfortable at Roma. I had two good seasons there and I was very happy. But I've always been the sort of guy who takes a chance, to put myself under pressure. Three years ago I didn't play much [for Chelsea], but since day one back in England I wanted to show what I can do. I think I'm doing well.'

He talked about Liverpool, the team with which he had played on his PlayStation as a boy: Sami Hyppiä, Jamie Carragher, Steven Gerrard ... how many games he had won thanks to the Reds captain? When they asked him if he was the new King of the Kop, he dodged the question: 'I can't say that, but I will leave it for the fans to say that, but I'm happy scoring goals for the club and that for me is the more important thing. We try to push ourselves to win something for us, for the fans, for the club, that's our target.' Mo talked about Klopp, describing him as a 'very nice guy' who is always trying to make his players happy, to help them give 100 per cent. He said that he considered him a friend from the outset, 'even if he is the manager and I'm the player. He asked me to always stay right in the middle of the action near the goal. You have to admit he knows how to make his strikers shine.' He described Mané and Firmino as 'top players' with whom he had a wonderful understanding: 'None of us are selfish, we try to bring the best out in one another to make things easier for us.' The number 11 also had his say about Coutinho: '[He is] a great man and a great player and I wish him all the best at his new club,' but he was also keen to point out that without Coutinho or even Salah himself, the team would still always try to give its best.

As far as could be judged from the first league game without Coutinho – against Pep Guardiola's Manchester City at Anfield on 14 January – the number 10's departure did not seem to have negatively affected the team. The Reds got their revenge for their previous meeting, beating the Citizens 4–3. But the Champions League was another thing entirely and the game against Porto at the Estádio do Dragão just a month later was a test away from home of life for the Reds without the Brazilian. It could not have gone better. Five-nil to Klopp's boys, who already had the quarter-finals in their sights. Mané scored a hat-trick, with Firmino and Mo getting one each. In the 29th minute, Milner's shot hit the post as the number 11 controlled the rebound with his foot and head like a performing seal before firing the ball into the back of the net.

Saturday, 17 March 2018, Anfield. Liverpool-Watford, in the snow, on the 31st matchday of the Premier League. The playing conditions were difficult and the pitch was slippery … but not for Mo Salah. The Egyptian was on fire!

In the fourth minute, Sadio Mané ran down the right wing before passing to the number 11 on the edge of the box; Mo then outfoxed two defenders, avoided a third and scored with his right foot. One-nil.

In the 43rd minute, Mané supplied Andy Robertson on the left, who put in a low, accurate cross. Mo popped up in timely fashion by the far post and anticipated the advancing Watford keeper Orestis Karnezis. Two-nil.

In the 49th minute, the number 11 was on the right wing. He jumped over a defender, picked up the ball by the touchline, looked up to see where his teammates were and provided Firmino with a perfect assist that the Brazilian back-heeled into the net. Three-nil.

In the 77th minute, Mané's cross found the dancing Momo, who wrong-footed four yellow-shirted opponents to find space and time to strike almost as he fell to the ground. Four-nil. But there was still more to come.

In the 85th minute, Salah supplied Danny Ings on the left. The number 28 unleashed a powerful shot that Karnezis fumbled. Who should get there first? Mo! Five-nil to Liverpool. Four for Salah, who walked off down the dressing room tunnel with the ball under his arm.

With his four strikes against Watford (coincidentally, the team against which he has scored in his first league game), Mo was on 28 Premier League goals and 36 in all competitions. He was the top scorer across Europe's five major leagues, surpassing Lionel Messi and Harry Kane. Comparisons with the Barcelona number 10 were inevitable; Klopp answered the question as follows: 'I don't think Mo wants to be compared with Lionel Messi. Messi has been doing what he's been doing for what feels like twenty years or so. The last player I know who had the same influence on a team performance was Diego Maradona. But Mo is in a fantastic way, that's for sure. As it always is in life, if you have to have the skills you have to show that constantly and consistently, and he is very good.'

What did the Man of the Moment have to say after his

exploits? In a post-match interview for BT Sport alongside Captain Jordan Henderson, he maintained his usual low profile. When they asked him how he felt having scored so many goals, including four for the first time in front of the Kop, he answered: 'I have to thank everyone, without my teammates I couldn't reach these numbers. Each game I want to score and help the team, but the three points are most important.' Three points were undoubtedly important because Mo dreamt of winning the Premier League with Liverpool, a title the club had not won for many, too many years, since the 1989–90 season to be precise, when England's top flight was still the First Division.

Mo scored the winning goal to see the Reds beat Crystal Palace in London in a league game on 31 March (2–1). He was the Premier League Player of the Month thanks to six goals in four games. It was the third time he had received the accolade, after winning in November and February, making him the first player to win it three times in a single season. The game against Palace came after the international break. On 23 March, Egypt played a friendly against Portugal in Zürich. It was billed as a showdown between Cristiano Ronaldo and Mohamed Salah, the two most in-form strikers in Europe. Victory went to the Portuguese, who overturned the result with two powerful headers in injury time, pulling the rug out from under the North Africans, who thought they had beaten the European champions. Mo Salah had given his team the lead in the 56th minute with a razor-sharp drive from the edge of the box. But, as everyone knows, CR7, captain of the team in red, never gives up. Despite the defeat, Héctor Cúper was happy with how his team had played, with the exception of the defensive blunders that had allowed the Portuguese to equalise. In the post-match press conference, he said of his number 10: 'I think Salah is one of the best players in the world at the moment and I don't know if he can be the best player in the world but what he's doing now is really important.'

Fourth of April 2018, the Anfield press room, about 11pm. Pep Guardiola, wearing a grey sweater pinned with a yellow bow (a symbol of solidarity with the imprisoned Catalan separatists), answered the first question asked by the assembled reporters. He gave his perspective on the game. It took barely a minute for an uncomfortable truth to come out: 'In this room there is no one except the guy who is talking to you who believes we are going to go through. Tomorrow we are going to try to convince ourselves this week that in six days we can work on our game and we still have 90 minutes.'

His Manchester City, who, three days earlier had passed up the chance to secure the Premier League title against United, had been given three firm slaps by Klopp and Co. It was their second defeat of the season at the hands of the Reds and it stung even more because it had come in the first leg of the Champions League quarter-final. The Reds had buried their opponents in 31 minutes of a fantastic first half of suffocating pressure and pace. And, of course, Mo Salah is a player who revels in those kind of scenarios. The Egyptian scored the first goal and provided an exquisite assist for Mané to head home to make it 3–0, Oxlade-Chamberlain bagging a memorable strike between the two. Mo was now on 38 appearances, with seventeen goals in his last fifteen official games. Devastating. It was a shame he had to leave the pitch in the 52nd minute with a muscle problem. There was plenty of concern in the stands. Klopp stepped up to provide reassurance: 'Mo says he's fine But we have to wait for a professional diagnosis.'

Three days later at Goodison Park, in a derby that would end in a goalless draw, Mo was not even on the pitch. But on 10 April, for the return leg of the Champions League quarter-final in Manchester, Mo stamped his card and helped scupper City's hopes of a comeback. In the 56th minute, the Citizens were 1–0 up. Off to a rocket of a start, Gabriel Jesus had breached Karius's goal in the second minute of the game. Pep Guardiola got himself sent to the stands by Spanish referee Antonio Mateu Lahoz after having words with the official in the wake of Leroy Sané's disallowed goal for offside. Liverpool's number 11 then stepped up in a state of grace to administer the decisive blow. Mané took on three defenders in the box but his shot was parried by Ederson. The move looked to be finished but instead Momo picked up the ball before Ederson could grab it and took it around the keeper. He celebrated by posing in the middle of the pitch with his arms out like Christ the Redeemer in Rio de Janeiro. Roberto Firmino later took care of finishing things off. 2–1. Pep said goodbye to the Champions League while the Reds went through to the semi-final.

Twenty-fourth of April 2018. Anfield and the Kop dedicated a prolonged standing ovation to Mohamed Salah as he left the pitch in the 75th minute, replaced by Danny Ings. They sang at the top of their voices: 'Mo Salah, running down the wing, Salah, Salah, Egyptian King.' The following day, the British press were in unison: 'The Mo-Show'; 'Sensational Salah'; 'Salah The Unstoppable'; 'Magic Mo downs Roma'; 'Mo Men 5 Romans 2'; 'DinaMO Kiev'; 'Greatest Mo on Earth.' Mo also dominated the Italian newspapers. 'Salah KOs Roma,' read the front page of the *La Gazzetta dello Sport*, alongside a photo of Momo with his hands together to beg forgiveness for his goals from the Romanista fans. *Il Corriere dello Sport* claimed 'the ex-Roma player did not take pity on his former teammates, giving his fans the umpteenth other-worldly performance of a season that is bringing him ever closer to the Ballon d'Or. Once the Egyptian King had gone off, however, everything changed. In the last ten minutes, Liverpool went back to being just a "normal" team.'

In addition to those directly involved, English winners and Italian losers, the international press also glorified Salah. He was described as 'dazzling' by the Spanish sporting daily *Marca*, while in France, *L'Équipe* spoke of an 'incredible year in which Salah has been living on a cloud', and *France Football* even awarded him a ten out of ten! Immense, monstrous, monumental, pure class, an extraordinary performance, an incredible night: there was no end to the epithets because, although he did not bear them a grudge, their former player had literally taken Roma apart in the first leg of the Champions League semi-final. The first blow, or the first stroke of genius, from the red-shirted number 11 came in the 35th minute. He received the ball from Firmino in the right-hand corner of the Roma area, took his time and unleashed a spinning left-footed shot that flew into the top corner of Alisson's goal. Unstoppable! In the 46th minute, the Egyptian did it again: he and Firmino led a perfect counterattack from the Reds. The Brazilian kindly gave him back the ball, which he delicately chipped over Alisson. It was the Egyptian's 43rd goal in a season in which he had made 47 appearances. And his match did not end there: he gifted the ball to Mané to make it 3–0 and then provided Firmino with an assist for 4–0. When Salah left the pitch, the scoreboard read 5–0 in Liverpool's favour. To get an idea of what was going on in Roman minds, you only had to look at the ashen-faced Francesco Totti, the former captain, once Salah's idol, who was watching from the stands.

But when it came to offering the hero of the night his stage, Klopp got his calculations wrong. Without their Egyptian, his team switched off and Roma clawed two back thanks to Džeko in the 80th minute and Perotti from the spot in the 85th. They could still hope for a miracle at the Olimpico. In Liverpool, there were plenty of regrets over the door left ajar to the Giallorossi's hopes when it should have been firmly slammed in their faces. Despite this, no one could deny that it was one of the greatest European nights in the history of Anfield, like the one against Saint-Étienne in 1977, Olympiakos in 2005, Real Madrid in 2009 or Borussia Dortmund in 2016. The only negative notes were the clashes outside the stadium that left Sean Cox, a Reds fan, in a coma and the serious injury to Oxlade-Chamberlain.

Two weeks later in Rome the Giallorossi almost repeated the exploits of the quarter-final when they had overturned the 4–1 result at the Camp Nou to dump Messi's Barcelona out of the competition. This time the wound was only a graze. With an extremely generous match, Roma won 4–2, but, thanks to the first leg result, it would be Liverpool going to the final in Kiev. Small consolation for the team managed by Eusebio di Francesco was the fact that they had stopped their former player from scoring and ended the Reds' unbeaten run in the competition.

Tenth of May 2018. Three awards in one night. The first two – 'Overall Player of the Season' and 'Players' Player of the Season' – were received by Salah at Anfield during the Liverpool Awards Dinner. In the official club suit, with the shield on his jacket and a red tie, he posed for photographers with the two trophies and reassured anyone who was worried that he would not be leaving at the end of the season, perhaps lured away by Real Madrid. 'I'm very happy here and everything is fine. I have got ambitions for the future with Liverpool. As you can see,' said Momo, 'we had a great season. It is just the beginning. We want to qualify for the Champions League next season and then we want to win the Champions League final. We will play to win against Real Madrid.'

Salah then flew to London, to the Landmark Hotel, where another award awaited him: the Football Writers' Association Footballer of the Year. Mo took the honour ahead of Kevin De Bruyne, the Manchester City midfielder, by fewer than twenty votes. Tottenham's Harry Kane came third. He was the first African to win football's oldest individual accolade, which was first awarded as long ago as 1948. In his role as host, Jürgen Klopp had had to stay at Anfield. But he did say this to the Football Writers' Association: 'There's not much I can say about what Salah "does on the pitch" that you guys haven't already seen and written about. The fact you have voted for him as your "player of the season" reflects that you have witnessed his incredible quality as a footballer. But it's his qualities as a person that should not be overlooked. I read and hear about him being a wonderful role model for Egypt, North Africa, for the wider Arabic world and for Muslims. This, of course, is true, but he is a role model full stop. Regardless of race or religion – country or region of birth. The only "labels" we should put on Mo is what a good person he is and what a fantastic footballer he is. And, by the way, the first part of that is more important in life than the second. Mo is someone who sets an example of how to approach life and how to treat others. Around Melwood, with his teammates and the club staff, he is gentle and humble despite being the international superstar he is now. The attention and acclaim has not changed him even by 0.01 per cent. He arrived at Liverpool humble and warm and this is the same boy who comes to be with you all tonight to accept your generous recognition. Although maybe a little more tired and weary of selfies and autographs, so keep that in mind please! Mo, we are very proud of you and thankful for what you have done for this team and club and of course we look forward to sharing many more seasons with you at Liverpool. In a season when Manchester City have been outstandingly good and played outstandingly well, football from another planet, you have won the two major awards. The one voted for by your fellow professionals and now the one voted for by the football writers. You are world class Mo, truly world class. And what's even more exciting, for you, for Liverpool, and for the public who get to watch you play: you can and will get even better. Congratulations my friend!"

There really is nothing to add.

Thirteenth of May 2018. The 38th and final matchday of the Premier League season. Liverpool, who needed one point to guarantee themselves fourth place in the table and a Champions League place for next season, did more than was required, beating Brighton at home, 4–0. Salah scored the first, taking him to a tally of 44 goals across all competitions. He beat the Premier League record as the first player to score 32 goals in a 38-game league. One more than the 31 scored by Alan Shearer (1995–95 season), Cristiano Ronaldo (2007–08) and Luis Suárez (2013–14). He was not far off the 47 goals scored by Ian Rush in the 1983–84 season, which ended with Liverpool winning the European Cup final against Roma at the Stadio Olimpico. He was two goals short of the 2017–18 European Golden Shoe award, which went, for the fifth time, to Lionel Messi for 34 goals in La Liga. When it came to the total number of goals scored during the season, the Egyptian was on a par with Cristiano

Ronaldo (44) and only had one fewer than Messi (45). He had had a record-breaking year, whichever way you looked at it: he was the African footballer who had scored the highest number of goals in a single season (beating Didier Drogba, who had scored 28 times for Chelsea in the 2009–10 season) and the most in the Champions League, and was also the top Egyptian scorer in the history of the Premier League.

What accounted for this avalanche of goals? What was behind this astonishing rise from a player who had worked miracles in just one season, become the King of Anfield, was being compared to two titans of the game like Messi and Ronaldo and was being given as 6–1 favourite to win the Ballon d'Or? There was no doubt that it was down to his hard work, footballing maturity and will to win in England, to show what he could do in a country where his football had previously failed.

It was important to remember that the boy from Nagrig had also found himself in a favourable environment; Klopp's footballing philosophy had helped him greatly. He had given him room to demonstrate his greatest gifts: pace, explosiveness, dribbling and goal-scoring instinct. Klopp's attacking flair had certainly been more useful to him than the typically Italian tactics employed by Luciano Spalletti. Thanks to the German's concept of dynamic team play – in which the striker works for the good of the team, but remains a striker – Salah had transformed himself into a goal-scoring machine alongside two others. It should not be forgotten that the Egyptian had found the perfect chemistry with Sadio Mané and Roberto Firmino. The Fab Three had scored a total of 89 times, 71 per cent of Liverpool's goals. They also showed themselves to be generous with one another and with the team: eight assists from the Senegalese, in addition to his nineteen goals; 27 goals and fourteen assists for the

Brazilian, plus fourteen assists for Salah to add to his goal tally. Fewer than De Bruyne (twenty) and Messi (eighteen) but plenty more than CR7 (seven). When it came to player of the week, month, year, Premier League or Africa, these record figures saw Salah win an astonishing 34 individual awards. The last of these, the Premier League's Golden Boot, was presented to him by Liverpool legend Kenny Dalglish on the turf at Anfield after the game against Brighton. Salah returned to the pitch holding the hand of Makka, his three-year-old daughter, who was wearing a replica red number 11 shirt. While Mo gave an interview and showed off his gold trophy to the fans, his little girl kicked a ball around. The stadium cheered her every touch and boos rang out when her dad came to take the ball from her. Let the children play, Momo! Your time to show what you can do will come in Kiev in just two weeks …

Chapter 18

Tears and anger

There's a party atmosphere in Madrid on this sunny, almost summery Saturday afternoon. Plenty of people are out in the streets, including tourists around the Prado Museum and the Puerto del Sol, Spain's kilometre zero. Work has been going on for some time in the Plaza de Cibeles, opposite the Palacio de Comunicaciones, the seat of the City Council and the former central post office; they are fencing off the fountain to protect the goddess Cybele from what might befall her later that night ... The square is filled with men and women wearing white T-shirts and scarves. Some have come from outside the city to soak up the atmosphere of the final, killing time wandering around the shops and department stores of Gran Vìa or in one of Madrid's many bars. As Joaquìn Sabina used to sing: 'In Anton Martìn [a Madrid square] alone, there are there more bars than in the whole of Norway!' From the most run-down to the shiniest and newest, every bar in Madrid is showing the final. But some are displaying signs that read 'We regret to say, Real Madrid-Liverpool tonight 8.45pm', run by Atlético Madrid fans who cannot bear to see the Merengues within touching distance of the biggest trophy in club football yet again. There are some, like the Shilote, who are taking telephone reservations to watch the Champions League final, with two drinks for €10 and a menu of arepas, nachos, tequeños, tacos, burritos and empanadas if anyone gets peckish while watching the match. As if a reminder was needed, the flyer shows an image of Salah alongside one of Cristiano Ronaldo. As far as the media are concerned, this is the key to the game.

In Malasaña – home to the Maravillas market and the 1980s nightlife district, the area immortalised in song by Juan Perro and turned into a brand by Manu Chao in *Me Gustas Tu* – the Triskel Tavern is bursting at the seams. And it's only 7pm. It's not an easy prospect getting through the throng of sweaty bodies, pints of beer and an orgy of red scarves and shirts, a veritable compendium of Liverpool history: Gerrard, Rush, Alonso, Torres, Mané, Firmino and Salah. No one is missing. A bearded man even holds up a huge green sash emblazoned with large letters: 'Paris 1981, Liverpool 1–0 Real Madrid, European Cup Final 27 May, Parc de Princes.' An auspicious reminder of the only previous final between the Reds and the Merengues, which Liverpool won thanks to a single goal from Alan Kennedy in the 81st minute.

It is almost impossible to get down the stairs to the basement because the underground entrance, between barrel vaults and exposed bricks, is reserved for the MadridReds, Liverpool's supporters club in the Spanish capital. They meet here regularly, in Calle de San Vicente Ferrer, in this Irish-style pub that has been run by two Leeds and Real Madrid fans for ten years. Every game is unmissable, as are reruns of past glories, featuring the likes of Ian Rush and Robbie Fowler. Today, 26 May 2018, everyone is here. No one wants to miss Liverpool's first Champions League final since 2007, when Rafa Benìtez and Steven Gerrard's team lost to Carlo Ancelotti and Kaká's AC Milan in Athens. Nor does anyone want to miss Mohamed Salah, the story of the season. 'Mo is magic. To start with, when he came, I thought they'd spent too much on a player that had failed at Chelsea and, despite playing well in Italy, had not really triumphed there either. But we've all had to change our minds. He's scored more than anyone would have dared to imagine and he could have got even more. I'm convinced he's going to score tonight,' predicts Chris from London. 'One for him and one for Mané. We're going to win 2–1.'

Fernando is an Atlético Madrid fan and is here to support the opposition. Real Madrid's opposition. 'Let's hope they lose. A third Champions League in a row would really be too much. Salah is one hell of a player.' Although I think it will be tough for him to repeat what he's done this season.'

Pietro from Brescia in Italy has also come to support the Merengues' opponents: 'They beat my team, Juve, in the quarter-finals, so it would be great to see Salah take the cup out of their hands.'

James, a Londoner transplanted to Madrid's Barrìo de la Letras, says that Real 'are favourites on paper. They have a better, more complete team with more experience in these kind of games, but we've got Salah, who can make the difference, like he has all season. It's going to be 3–2 to us.'

'No, I wouldn't swap Salah for Cristiano Ronaldo. I like Mo as a person and as a player because he's adapted well to Klopp's game, because he's had an exceptional season and because … before he came to Madrid, Ronaldo was at United,' explains Javi.

Patricia, wearing an obligatory red shirt, has come to watch the game with a friend. She is a Salah fan; she thinks he has an incredible smile and is cool.

Charles, from Bordeaux, fell in love with the Reds when he was a boy because they represent the history of football, or rather he fell in love with the Kop and its fans. He is on holiday in Spain but was not going to miss the final. He is convinced that Liverpool can do it and that Salah can pick apart the Blancos' defence.

Tomas is sure that in Liverpool Salah has found the place to become one of the greats; he says: 'I only hope he will stay with Klopp for another couple of years so he can get even better.'

As the minutes pass, the atmosphere heats up as the singing and drinking continue. No different from a pub on the Anfield Road just before a game. There is still an hour to go until kick-off but there's no more room at the Triskel Tavern. At this point, fans have to content themselves with standing outside, peering through the window for an average view of one of the big screens at best. The two teams are waiting in the tunnel; we see a close-up of Salah, scrutinised at first-hand by Cristiano Ronaldo. Out on the pitch, Mo prays while Jürgen Klopp says a hasty hello to Zinedine Zidane, the Real manager. A roar welcomes every name delivered by the announcer, getting even louder for Momo. Cristiano Ronaldo and Sergio Ramos are greeted by whistles. 'You'll Never Walk Alone' rings out around Kiev's Olympic Stadium and Madrid's Triskel Tavern.

8.45pm James Milner kicks off.

In only the 23rd second, an extremely quick Raphaël Varane beats Mané to it; Salah has already put him through into the box.

In the second minute. Cristiano Ronaldo is offside as he tries to chase down a ball from Luka Modrić. Loris Karius punches it away regardless.

In the third minute, Varane stops a shot from Georginio Wijnaldum just outside the box. Salah was lying in wait.

In the fifth minute, Marcelo fouls Salah as he tries to take the ball off him from behind.

In the sixth minute, an extremely alert Modrić blocks a shot from Salah.

In the seventh minute, Firmino sends the ball deep for Mané but a sliding Varane gets there first. The ball flies up towards the advancing Keylor Navas but Marcelo clears it before Salah can take it.

In the eighth minute, Salah comes again. He gets the ball from Alexander-Arnold before finding Firmino on the edge of the box. The Brazilian knocks it back with his head, but Ramos gets to it and Navas has to rush out to stop Salah and Alexander-Arnold getting involved.

In the eleventh minute, Marcelo gets free of Milner and tries a long-distance strike. The poor shot ends up a long way from Karius.

In the twelfth minute, Madrid hold onto the ball, trying to calm things down, staying in their own half.

In the thirteenth minute, Mané passes to Salah in the middle of the box. Despite being surrounded by three white shirts, the number 11 shoots but the rebound falls to Mané, whose shot is turned away by Casemiro. It then comes back to the feet of Firmino, who is stopped by Dani Carvajal.

In the fourteenth minute, Keylor Navas punches away a shot from Alexander-Arnold. Madrid are under the cosh.

In the fifteenth minute, a first chance for Ronaldo. Carvajal passes to the Portuguese player, who speeds down the wing and into the box but fires over the crossbar due to the tight angle.

In the eighteenth minute, Momo takes a corner from the right. Navas flails as Van Dijk beats Varane to it at the far post but heads over the bar.

In the 22nd minute, Ramos picks up a long ball from the Reds, looking for Firmino in a dangerous position.

In the 23rd minute, Milner goes on a run down the left

wing and crosses into the box for Firmino. The Brazilian is slow to turn around and his shot is blocked by Sergio Ramos; the ball flies away but ends up at the feet of Trent Alexander-Arnold, whose powerful right-footed shot draws an impressive save from Keylor Navas.

Liverpool are pressing, picking up balls in the opposition half, dominating and creating dangerous chances. So far, they are spectacular. Their final could not have got off to a better start. The pub is deafened by applause and cheers.

8.11pm, 25 minutes into the first half. Just inside the Madrid half, Salah controls the ball with his head to keep the move going, but Sergio Ramos grabs him by the left arm, almost in a judo hold, pulls him down and falls on top of him. The referee stays silent. Isco speeds off with the ball as Momo is crying in pain on the ground. Ramos comes over, gives him a pat on the side and calls the referee. The game is stopped. Other Madrid players come over to Salah as he points to his left shoulder. Fans are holding their breath in the Triskel Tavern, at Kiev's Olympic Stadium, in Liverpool, Nagrig and across Egypt.

8.13pm, the 27th minute of the game. Salah is on his feet; it looks as if he is going to be able to continue, although his face is a mask of pain.

8.15pm, the 29th minute. Salah is down again. He can't go on.

8.16pm, the 30th minute. Mohamed Salah leaves the field in tears. First Mané, then Cristiano Ronaldo try to console him. Accompanied by Rubens Pons, Liverpool's Spanish physio, he walks towards Klopp before disappearing into the belly of the stadium.

In the 31st minute, Adam Lallana, the number 20, comes on for the number 11.

The insults thrown at Sergio Ramos in the Madrid pub

cannot be repeated. It is a cruel end to such a dream season. And everyone in the pub knows it.

'We knew it was something serious as soon as he fell on the ground because he never complains. We feared the worst,' Pons would tell *Marca* a few days later. 'We stayed at the stadium until half-time. Momo was devastated,' continues the physio. 'I tried to keep him calm. I told him he couldn't do anything about it now and that he should not worry. It was time to look for solutions and not regret that things had not worked out.' At half-time, Salah and Pons go to the nearest hospital for tests. The match continues; they follow it on social media and the security guard who has gone with them keeps them updated. Karim Benzema scores thanks to a terrible mistake by Karius. Mané equalises but then Gareth Bale pulls off an amazing bicycle kick to make it 2–1. Mané hits the post but butterfingers Karius delivers another howler, failing to hold on to a long-range shot from Bale. Three-one to Real Madrid and a third consecutive Champions League for Zidane and Co. There are no celebrations at Madrid's Triskel Tavern. The white-shirted fans prepare for a long night and mount an assault on the Plaza de Cibeles, where the Merengues' victories are always celebrated. Jürgen Klopp has his say in the post-match press conference in Kiev: 'We started well and played exactly as we wanted to play. The situation with Ramos and Mo, it was a shock for the team. We lost our positive momentum. Half-time, came in, and then what can I say about the goals. We scored one, they scored three, that's the result. Mo's World Cup place is in doubt. He would have played on if he could. I think he's in hospital at the moment having an X-ray. It doesn't look good.'

Once the tests are complete, Salah and Pons return to the stadium, but by now the game has long since finished. The Reds are about to get back on the team bus. 'We had to help

Mo change as he couldn't do it on his own, then we went to the airport,' explains Pons. Local TV pictures show Salah with his left arm in a sling. The initial diagnosis points to a dislocated shoulder, a lesion that will probably rule him out of the World Cup, which, for Egypt, starts in just twenty days.

Mohamed Salah tries to be optimistic, tweeting: 'It was a very tough night, but I'm a fighter. Despite the odds, I'm confident that I'll be in Russia to make you all proud. Your love and support will give me the strength I need.'

The next day, a treatment schedule is drawn up in agreement with doctors from the Egyptian national side. Three or four week's recovery time, but physios and other medical staff commit to doing everything possible to reduce this. On 29 May, Mohammed Salah flies to Valencia to be treated by Pons. He is intercepted at the airport by a journalist from the Spanish TV programme *Jugones*, who fires questions at him: 'Will you play at the World Cup? Do you think Ramos did it on purpose? Would you move to Real Madrid if an offer came in?' It makes no difference. Momo, wearing a shirt with horizontal stripes and a black hood, smiles but refuses to answer even the most trivial of questions: 'How are you? Lots of people are worried about you.' Mo's countrymen make up for the silence and they are not alone. There is plenty being said on Egyptian social media: 'A man fell on his shoulder and 100 million people felt the pain,' writes Mohamed Shawky on Twitter, adding a broken heart emoji. 'Every Muslim in the world is making *dua* [a Muslim prayer] against Ramos now,' tweets @musskkaayy. 'I swear, Sergio Ramos, we will get what is our right from you,' adds the Egyptian billionaire Naguib Sawaris. 'Good morning. May God burn you with gasoline Ramos you dog,' writes Hameed Farouq, a talent show producer, with no holds barred. The hashtag #*ibn_wasja* (son of a bitch) is trending, along with

Ramos_kalb (Ramos, dog), a very offensive insult in Arabic. Hundreds of tweets advise the Madrid captain against setting foot in Egypt for the foreseeable future. Bassem Whaba, an Egyptian lawyer, files a lawsuit against FIFA asking Ramos for €1 billion in compensation 'for having deliberately inflicted physical and psychological damage on an entire nation and its most famous footballer.'

An online petition through Change.org demands that: 'UEFA and FIFA should take measures against Ramos and similar players, using the video recordings of matches to keep the spirit of the game.' It is signed by more than half a million people. But there are also those who, instead of taking the Real Madrid captain to task, blame Salah for breaking the Ramadan fast. Kuwaiti preacher Mubarak al-Bathali claims on Twitter that 'God punished him for eating and drinking to be able to play in a football match. This is not a legitimate excuse. Life is in the hands of God and everything happens according to his will. Perhaps the injury was a good thing. Salah is a virtuous man, good and respected as an ambassador for Islam in the West. Do not grieve, the door of repentance is open.' Al-Bathali's opinion does not find favour. As far as the Egyptian media are concerned, Ramos is responsible. For example, the *Al-Masry Al-Youm* headline beneath a photo of Salah in tears reads: 'The night Egyptians cried: Ramos the butcher dislocated Abu Salah's shoulder.' The online journal *Youm7* publishes a cartoon with the caption: 'The devil Ramos kills Salah's dreams.'

On 5 June, while at a training camp with the Spanish national side, Sergio Ramos defends himself against the accusations: 'Lots of stories have been written about Salah. I didn't want to talk about it because in the end, it gets magnified, but looking closely at the play, he grabs my arm first and I fall the other way. He hurts his other arm, but then people are saying it was a judo move.' In addition to insisting it was an accident, he adds: 'I sent him a message and he's doing well.' The Seville-born player then goes on to claim that if Salah 'had had an injection, he could even have played the second half. I've done it a few times, it wasn't such a big deal.'

Salah's answer, or rather answers, come three days later in an interview with *Marca*. Hugo Cerezo asks him:

'Do you think it was normal?'

'I don't know. Maybe?'

'What do you think about what Ramos said?'

'It's funny.'

'Do you agree when Sergio said if you'd had an injection you could have played the second half?'

'My comment is that it's always OK when the one who made you cry first then makes you laugh. Maybe he could also tell me if I'm going to be ready for the World Cup?'

Chapter 19

Two goals are not enough

The sun is setting. The half-built brick houses that surround the ramshackle football pitch are tinged with gold, then orange, and finally an intense red. Night falls suddenly. The muezzin at the mosque beyond calls the faithful to prayer. Four boys are kicking a ball about; another rides around them on a bike. The youngest are playing chase. Two men, one leaning on a 1970s motorcycle and the other wearing an immaculate *jellabiya*, are chatting by the entrance to Nagrig's Mohamed Salah Youth Centre. Inside, in the large hall on the ground floor, they have been working for hours to set up cables, speakers and a big screen to show Egypt's second game at the 2018 World Cup. It is Tuesday 19 June; the Pharaohs face Russia in Saint Petersburg in a match that could see the hosts qualify for the knock-out stage. Four days earlier in Yekaterinburg, Héctor Cúper's team in red lost 1–0 to Luis Suárez and Edinson Cavani's Uruguay. As things stand in Group A, Egypt have still to score any points, compared with the three already posted by the South Americans and the host nation.

Before the game against the Celeste, Cúper had provided reassurance that, barring any unforeseen circumstances, Salah would be on the pitch, but in the end he did not come on for even a minute; Mo watched Diego Godín's winning header from the bench. The Argentine manager later explained that Salah had not played because 'we did not want to expose him to any risk or danger. His recovery is proceeding as normal and we believe he will be able to play in the next game.' His time has come against Russia. In Nagrig and across the country, 100 million people are waiting for him to be their Saviour, the man who can change destiny. Even the Russians want him on the pitch because, according to Stanislav Cherchesov, their manager: 'Salah is the kind of player who lights up tournaments like this. Not just in Egypt but for the whole world.' There is no doubt that, like Cristiano Ronaldo, Lionel Messi and Antoine Griezmann, he is one of the most hotly anticipated stars of Russia 2018. He is the striker who scored 44 goals at Liverpool and sent Anfield into raptures. He is the number 10 who has scored 33 goals in an Egypt shirt. He is the player who converted a penalty in the 94th minute to take Egypt to their first World Cup in 28 years. He is the most popular player in the Arab world and the most famous Arab personality on the planet. The British Museum even celebrated him as a modern icon of Egypt and put his mint green football boots on display in Room 61, a gallery in which other exhibits include a wall painting from the tomb-chapel of Nebamun.

Brandan Bmike Odums, an American artist, painted him with a saintly halo on the side of a building just around the corner from New York's Times Square. Ahmed Fathy immortalised a smiling Mo next to the Zahret Al Bustan Café in downtown Cairo, just across from portraits of Egypt's greats, such as Umm Kulthum, the singer, Naguib Mahfouz, the Nobel Prize winner, and Ahmed Fouad Negm, the poet. In the run-up to the World Cup, Salah's face was everywhere in Egypt: from votive Ramadan candles to large billboards, from replica national team strip printed with a number 10 to T-shirts simply emblazoned with the word Egypt. Plenty of songs have also been written about him;

there is even a rap by La Fouine, the French-Moroccan musician.

Expectation for the Egyptian King is huge, but for Salah the World Cup in Russia has been and will continue to be far from easy. In ways that have nothing to do with his injury. The first controversy, or rather the first conflict of interests, began in April. Momo has a sponsorship deal with Vodafone and the telecoms company launched an incredible promotion in March 2018: eleven minutes of free calls for every goal scored by the Liverpool number 11. Similarly, the Egyptian Federation is sponsored, among others, by WE, the mobile service of Telecom Egypt and a direct competitor of Vodafone. WE used images of Salah for its billboards and various forms of advertising. The most visible of these was the face of the number 10 on the fuselage of the Egypt Air plane used by the national team to travel to away games. A campaign paid for by WE. Salah was furious, describing the affair as 'a major insult'. His agent, Ramy Abbas, launched a social media blitz on Twitter with the hashtag #ISupportMohamedSalah. There was even talk of Mo boycotting Russia 2018 entirely. Eventually, Minister of Youth and Sports Khaled Abdel-Aziz got involved in the controversy, summoning the board members of the Egyptian Football Association for urgent talks and assuring 'everyone that we will stand by [Salah] and help him honour all the contracts he has entered into in England. We will meet all the demands made by Salah and his agent.'

The second row involved Chechen leader Ramzan Kadyrov.

Egypt's decision to choose Chechnya, a Muslim country, as the location for its team's World Cup base was strongly criticised by Human Rights Watch. Jane Buchanan, director of the NGO that advocates on human rights, described it as 'absolutely shocking and outrageous.' She lobbied FIFA to move the base to another city. As far as HRW were concerned, authorising this decision would be tantamount to legitimising the regime of Kadyrov, a puppet of Putin who rules Chechnya with a ruthless grip. He is suspected of crimes against humanity, such as kidnapping, summary executions, the murder of opponents and journalists, torture and illegal detentions. He is also accused of persecuting LGBT people, detained in secret prisons, tortured and in some cases killed.

FIFA did not reverse its decision, nor did the EFA, and Kadyrov, a big football fan who has played in exhibition matches with the likes of Diego Maradona and Totò Schillaci, took advantage of the presence of a global football star like Mohamed Salah. He reportedly went to pick him up at the hotel and drove him to the stadium where the Egyptian national team were training, taking the opportunity to be filmed and photographed with Momo in front of 8,000 fans. He also hijacked the event to make pro-Putin statements, claiming that the organisation of the World Cup had been a success despite attempts at sabotage by the 'enemies of Russia', going on to assert that 'Putin has shown that there is nothing our great country, Russia, cannot do.' On 15 June, Salah's birthday, Kadyrov presented Mo with a 100 kilogram-cake with 26 candles in the colours of the Egyptian and Chechen flags, topped by a golden boot. And there was more to come … During a sumptuous banquet in the presidential palace, Kadyrov made Salah an honorary citizen of the Chechen Republic. All these photos, cake and honours triggered quite the controversy. Kadyrov had used sport as propaganda to perfection and Salah found himself caught in the middle. Someone who is always so careful to remain apolitical had been exploited. CNN even claimed that he was on the verge of retiring from international football before the last group game. This was immediately denied by the Egyptian Federation, who cried 'fake news' and said Salah was happy, eating dinner and laughing with his teammates. But the shadow of doubt remained.

There was still one more row between Mo and the EFA to come, this time about security. The training base in Grozny and the hotel in Saint Petersburg had been transformed into a circus or, as one commentator described it, 'into a village wedding ceremony'. 'We had many disturbances at the team's camp,' Salah would later write. 'I couldn't go to the restaurant twice as they told me you won't be able to go there for your own safety due to the crowd inside the hotel.' He added that he had been bothered several times by guests coming to his room, wanting to say hello and talk to him.

The same thing happened in Saint Petersburg, when, the night before the crunch game against Russia, an entire celebrity delegation of businessmen, entrepreneurs, sportspeople, journalists, TV presenters, actors and dancers turned up on a trip sponsored by WE that caused endless debate. 'Every company has the right to sponsor stars to travel, but why are they all staying so close to a team that is supposed to be in a state of focus and readiness?' asked Egyptian columnist Yasser Ayoub on Twitter. Salah and Abbas would continue to be caught up in this diatribe on security and image rights until well after the end of the World Cup. Liverpool's number 11 tweeted: 'It's normal that a football federation seeks to solve the problems of its players so they can feel comfortable. But in fact, what I see is exactly the opposite. It is not normal that my messages and my lawyer's messages are ignored. Do you not have time to respond to us?!'

But let's leave the controversies to one side and get back to Nagrig at 7.30pm on 19 June. The hall at the youth centre is full to bursting. Men of all ages and kids are trying to sneak in everywhere. On streets across the country, where, until a few hours beforehand, quiet reigned supreme, impromptu 'fan zones' have sprung up. These have nothing to do with the initiative put in place by Vodafone for the Champions League final; people have simply organised them on their own. In a place that hosted a wedding celebration earlier in the afternoon, there is now a screen and rows of occupied seats on the dirt ground, with veiled women standing at the back. The cafés have done the same, bringing their TV sets out into the street. There is a real party atmosphere. A country is waiting for its hero.

The youth centre hall is now completely full. Those still trying to get in say hello to the foreigners, not often seen in these parts, before looking for a seat or climbing up for a glimpse of the view from outside. When Salah makes his entrance in a white number 10 shirt liberation comes, a cry of joy as his name is called.

But straight away there's a feeling that Salah is playing because Egypt need him but that he is not at 100 per cent. He is playing with the handbrake on, floating around on the margins of the action, saving his efforts and maximising the moments when his teammates manage to find him unmarked. This is not the usual Salah, with his explosive pace and raids down the wing, the player no one can contain when he's playing in a Liverpool shirt. Seemingly anxious in his early one-on-ones, he tries to avoid contact with the Russian defenders as much as possible. By the end of the first half, he is the Egyptian player who has had the least time on the ball. In part because as soon as he gets it he is immediately surrounded by three opponents but also because the midfielders in white can't quite seem to do their job properly. He is picked up twice at the far post but leaves the Egyptian fans with their hearts in their mouths when, in the 42nd minute, a dummy from Marwan Mohsen finds him on the edge of the box. Momo pivots between two defenders and kicks a spinning ball that flies just a few inches wide. Five minutes later, to the great disappointment of the assembled crowd in the hall, Russia are lucky to take the lead. El-Shenawy punches away a cross from the left but it falls to Roman Zobnin, who connects poorly with the ball 25 yards out. Ahmed Fathy, the Egyptian captain, attempts a clearance but deflects the ball into his own net with his right foot, unwittingly sending his keeper the wrong way.

At half-time the people of Nagrig remain in their seats. Hoping. But in the Krestovsky Stadium the red-shirted Russians take control, sinking the Pharaohs in the space of three minutes. First, Denis Cheryshev makes it 2–0 in the 59th minute by beating el-Shenawy from the six-yard line, then Artem Dzyuba makes it 3–0 in the 62nd minute. No one leaves the Nagrig youth centre despite the fact that, by this stage, Egypt have little hope of making a comeback. Their only happiness comes from seeing Mohamed Salah score. In the 72nd minute, the number 10 is manhandled by Zobnin in the box. Penalty! Confirmed by VAR. Momo fires home a powerful shot under the bar and Igor Akinfeev is beaten. The goal is celebrated like a victory here in Nagrig. But it is too late for the Pharaohs. In the post-match press conference, Héctor Cúper admits that Egypt have almost zero chance of qualifying, but he says that 'we will try to fin- ish the World Cup in the best way possible.' As for Salah, he explains: 'I was told he was feeling good. Of course, he could not prepare with us in the training camp and had to train alone so that might mean his total physical condition may have been reduced. I think he was OK. If he had not injured himself in the Champions League final then he would have had an extra three weeks to train with us. We all know what he means for the squad. He is a vital player – the focal point – and has given the team a great satisfaction. He suffered an injury and we have all been worried about it. We would have all preferred his injury to not occur. I would have liked him to be present in the training camps but the priority for him was to recover from his shoulder injury and have him available as soon as possible. We didn't have him available against Uruguay but did today and that was not enough.'

The following day, the Egyptian press take Cúper to task ('resign and Allah will forgive you'), praising Salah 'the good son of Egypt who wanted to play despite still being injured and scored the first World Cup goal in 28 years.' Disappointment at the defeat can be read on his face as he talks of a team that 'held firm in the first half but was swept away in the second by three Russian goals.'

On Monday 25 June at the Volgograd Arena, Egypt play their last World Cup game against Saudi Arabia, who conceded five against Russia in the opening game and lost 1–0 to Uruguay. Strangely, the name Mo Salah does not appear on the original team sheet tweeted by the Egyptian FA before the game. Speculation mounts as to whether the number 10 really did intend to retire from international football after the Grozny debacle. The federation later explains that this was a simple mistake; Mo would in fact be on the pitch. He even gives his team the lead in the 22nd minute. A long ball from Abdallah Said in midfield picks out Salah between two green-shirted defenders on the edge of the box. Three touches and it's a goal. The first two to control the ball and the third to create a beautiful chip that goes over the head of the advancing Yasser Al-Mosailem. Momo falls to his knees to celebrate. One-nil.

Three minutes later, he has a golden opportunity to double Egypt's lead. One-on-one with the Saudi keeper, he chips him yet again, but this time the ball fails to find its way to the back of the net and rolls behind. The spotlight shifts to Essam el-Hadary, the Pharaohs' veteran keeper, who, in the 40th minute, excels himself by saving a penalty from Faha Al-Muwallad. But he can't do it a second time. In the 50th minute, he is beaten by Salman Al-Faraj, who makes no mistake from the spot. One-one at the end of a first half that has nevertheless seen an active Salah, dangerous up front and combining well with Trezeguet. But in the second half, Momo runs out of steam as Egypt are forced to defend and have a fantastic performance from el-Hadary to thank for keeping them on level terms. But in injury time, the Saudis find the winning goal from Salem Al-Dawsari. Two-one and they get the better of the Pharaohs. Salah goes out of the World Cup with just two goals that have meant little. 'Maybe he wasn't able to do what he normally does, what we're used to, but he scored. Maybe we could have expected more but he isn't the only one. He needs help and support from his teammates,' Cúper says after the game. And when they ask him if his number 10 really is going to retire from international football, he answers with amazement: 'I don't think so. I don't think it's true because all those who are here, and lots who couldn't come, really appreciate the opportunity to play for their country.'

Voted FIFA Man of the Match, Momo does not attend the press conference and fails to collect his award. He walks through the mixed zone without stopping to talk to the journalists with their many questions. He would later tell the beIN Sport microphones: 'I thank Egyptian fans for our support during the World Cup. I know it is difficult for them but it was also difficult for us.' He explains the debacle by saying: 'The Egyptian team does not have prior experience of the World Cup. We reached the cup for the first time after 28 years of absence. The players did their best and I am sure that the future will be better.' Salah's future will be the Egyptian national side and Liverpool.

On 2 July, he signs a new contract keeping him at the Merseyside club until 2023. The financial details are kept secret but Salah is thought to be going to double his salary to £200,000 a week. The lack of a release clause also puts Liverpool in a powerful position against other clubs such as Real Madrid, who are interested in the number 11. Jürgen Klopp, back at Melwood to start pre-season training, has the following to say: 'I think this news can be seen for what it is: rewarding a person who performed and contributed greatly for the team and the club last season. It demonstrates two things very clearly also, his belief in Liverpool and our belief in him. When someone like Mo Salah commits and says this place is my home now, it speaks very loudly, I think. Equally, our commitment to him says we see his value and want him to grow even more and get even better within our environment.'

Hamdy Nouh, Mo's second father, must also be happy. He was delighted that at Liverpool his player had 'met a good coach who knows how to improve his gifts'.

Chapter 20

Hope

He smiles. From ear to ear. Pointing up to the sky before kneeling down on the pitch to thank Allah whenever he scores. He is religious and a good Muslim. He doesn't drink or smoke and respects the fast but is crazy about *kushari*, a dish made from rice, macaroni, lentils, chickpeas, garlic and a spiced tomato sauce. Whenever his friends bring it over for him from Egypt he devours it in the car, with his hood up so as not to be recognised. He does not talk a lot. He is relatively shy and reserved. He uses social media in moderation and does not grant many interviews. His comments never veer into dangerous territory. Away from the stadium, he has a normal life with Makka, Magi and his family, far from the bright lights and media buzz of the glittering world of football. He does not have any tattoos, doesn't dye or bleach his hair nor have it cut into a Mohican. He is generous: he devotes time and money to charity, compensating for the shortcomings of the Egyptian state. The only stands he has taken are the refusal to shake the hands of the Maccabi Tel Aviv players and the number 74 shirt he wore in honour of the victims of the Port Said riot. All in all, it can be said that Mohamed Salah is a quiet, humble guy who does not stray from the straight and narrow, has not revolutionised the world and does not make explosive statements. Yet, in a short time, a very short time, he has become a positive role model on a global scale. And that is not all … Unlike other

sporting heroes and role models who have won over teen-
agers around the world, political, social and religious values
have been assigned to Salah. He is the subject of debate,
essays, accusations and endless accolades. And not for what
he does with the ball at his feet, but for what he represents
in the eyes of millions. Paraphrasing Tom Goodyear, author
of the essay 'Mohamed Salah and The Political Power of the
Apolitical Entertainer', Salah the idea is more important
than Salah the football player.

Let's start in his native land. Paradoxically, Salah has
become a political voice despite never talking about politics. He is not Didier Drogba, who asked Ivorians to lay
down their arms and organise elections live on TV to the
nation in 2006. Nor is he Muhammad Ali, who refused to
fight in Vietnam, or Tommie Smith and John Carlos, who
raised black-gloved fists to protest against racism and injus-
tice against African-Americans in the United States at the
1968 Mexico Olympics. He is not a politician, yet during
Egypt's 2018 presidential elections Salah received a million
votes. No one may have actually checked the ballot papers
on which the names of el-Sisi and Moussa Mostafa Moussa
were scrubbed out and overwritten with 'Mohamed Salah,
President,' but, despite remaining legend, this does demonstrate the importance of a figure who has reunified a country
divided between liberals and nationalists, revolutionaries and
counter-revolutionaries, civilians and military, those for and
against the Muslim Brotherhood, and those for and against
the regime. A country that has lived against and not for.

'Salah operates in a politics of juxtaposition in which his
perceived immaculate persona is unconsciously contrasted
with the familiar polluted forces of high politics,' writes
Amro Ali, an analyst and associate professor of sociology at
the American University of Cairo in his essay 'Unhappiness

and Mohamed Salah's Egypt.' Ali goes on to add: 'The intervention of Salah did not necessarily change all that, nor did it reverse the Orwellian trend, but he did help restore meaning to terms that had become scrambled: dignity became dignity again, principles became principles, kindness became kindness, and happiness became happiness.'

In Salah, Egyptians have found an impartial figure who inspires respect and trust. Momo is aware of this and is proud to be a role model. 'What would my message be? With self-confidence, sacrifice, work and perseverance, you can improve your life. It worked for me, so it can work for you. Always believe in yourself,' he tells *L'Équipe Magazine*.

A simple message, but one that responds to the need for new words, new ideas, new faces, new ways of thinking and doing after other men have died, left or disappointed all expectations. It responds to the search for a positive hero who, by leading his own life as an example, as one of them, offers young people and others the hope that shattered into a thousand pieces after the dreams of the 2011 revolution. Hope in a country suffering from poverty, unemployment, austerity measures imposed by the IMF, galloping inflation, corruption, repression, lack of freedom, censorship and terrorism. Salah gives his compatriots back dignity and pride in being Egyptian, being free, strong and recognised on an international level.

These 'political' values have been exploited by advertising, such as Vodafone's commercial made for the Arab market. One minute and 37 seconds in which Momo appears playing with his daughter, training, walking through the streets of Liverpool and looking around Anfield. But it also features his fans, Egyptian and English, kids playing in his shirt, the effigy of the number 10 stuck on a pram, in a bar or on the dashboard of a car. The voice over, in Arabic, narrates: 'Only one person has been able to rally all these people behind him. He made them connect with him and support him as he became hope for them. He created a scenario that cannot be explained. And they created a hero that cannot be replaced … Their love for him is real … They see themselves in him. He is an exact copy of them. Although there are millions of them and he is only one. Their son. From them. From their spirits. Even though he is in a foreign land they still expect everything that's good to come from him … What's strange and beautiful at the same time is that a whole nation sees itself in just one person: Mohamed Salah. He has returned our joy to us. He made us believe that if we unite behind something we become stronger than anything else.'

Similarly, his value in a social context has been exploited by the Ministry of Social Solidarity and the Fund for Drug Control and Treatment of Addiction (FDCTA): Momo appears at the end of a video advising 'Say NO to Drugs!' followed by a rehab hotline number. When this campaign was shared on various social media channels by 120 million followers, calls to the drugs helpline rose by 400 per cent!

He also has a religious value to the Muslim world. Salah does not hide his faith, demonstrating it in public despite now being a global star. He is not ashamed to pray before a game in front of thousands of spectators. He is not embarrassed to walk with his wife in a headscarf across the Anfield pitch. He does it simply, bringing religion back to its simple and natural state. Al-Azhar, one of Sunni's Islam's most prestigious study centres claims that 'Salah's success and prostrations are a triumph of religion.' But this opinion is vehemently opposed by Ahmed Khaled, author of *Mo*, an Egyptian biography of Salah, who wonders: 'For what religion would it be that triumphs through a football player?

Can Messi or Ronaldo's excellence be considered a triumph for Christianity?' The debate is an extremely heated one.

Salah's impact is not confined to his native land. He has contributed more to spreading a positive image of Egypt than endless marketing campaigns, conferences and meetings of the World Tourism Organisation. Of course, it is not just advertising and anti-drugs initiatives that are making the most of Mo, the regime is too. In January 2017, a photo appeared of him standing next to President Abdel Fattah el-Sisi and Minister of Youth and Sport Khaled Abdel Aziz. El-Sisi had received whole teams before but never a single player. The president congratulated Momo on his results for the national team, as well as for the awards he had received. He thanked him for his contribution of 5 million Egyptian pounds (£200,000 GBP) to the Tahya Masr (Long Live Egypt) fund to strengthen the economy. In April, following Liverpool's victory over Roma, el-Sisi posted the following on his Facebook page: 'I would like to congratulate the son of Egypt, Mohamed Salah, for his goals [that] underline the abilities of Egyptians in all fields. I am proud of him and all Egyptians who hold the name of Egypt high.'

Also in April, it seems it was the president who intervened to resolve the dispute between Salah and the federation over image rights. On 27 May, the day after Mo's injury in the Champions League final, the president called the Liverpool number 11. He later announced to the country on his social media account: 'I made contact with Egypt's son and my son, Mohamed Salah, to check on him after the injury. As I expected, I found him a champion, stronger than the injury and excited for the journey. I have asserted to him that he has become an Egyptian icon of pride and glory.' He concluded by saying: 'I pray to Allah, from a father to his son, for his quick recovery and to protect him.' This post provoked a range of reactions, some followers praised the president for supporting a national hero, while others believed el-Sisi was using Salah for purely political ends. And he was not the only one … The Egyptian Football Association, which openly supported the re-election of the president, not only used Salah's image in a way that angered him but also involved him in the Chechen affair and its resulting controversy.

But who will Salah be in Egypt after the fiasco of the World Cup? Will he still be able to be the symbol of hope for a people, the hero of an unhappy country, or will discontent prevail? It does not seem like it judging by the Cairo crowd that gathered at the number 10's house for autographs and selfies when his address was leaked on Facebook. But it may yet prove to be more complicated. Take the cartoon drawn by the Egyptian cartoonist Andeel. It shows a man desperately clinging to the ground so as not to sink into a chasm as the studs of a football boot stamp down hard on his arm, threatening his last grip. The man is angry. Could this be the end of a dream shared by millions of people?

European and Arab commentators alike are wondering what will happen to Salah after Hany Abo Rida, president of the Egyptian Football Association, blamed the Muslim Brotherhood for the Pharaohs' poor performance in the pages of *Al-Watan*. In March, Salah Montasser said in an article in *Al-Ahram* that Mo should shave off his beard because: 'Although his beard does not put him on a list of terrorists, it does include him among those who sympathise with them,' or with the Muslim Brotherhood, declared an illegal terrorist organisation in 2013. Will Momo suffer the same fate as that which befell his idol Mohamed Aboutrika, 'The Magician', the number 22, his former teammate in the national side? Aboutrika, who supported the candidacy of Mohamed Morsi and protested against the Rabaa massacre, was accused of financing the Muslim Brotherhood in 2015. His assets were seized and he was forced to flee to Qatar. He has been on a terrorist watch list since 2017 and the Cairo Criminal Court extended his sentence for another five years in May 2018. He risks immediate arrest if he tries to return to Egypt. It is a sad story for a former champion, an idol who for many was the best player in Africa, adored by his people. The lesson that Salah may have learned from his idol to survive is to maintain a conciliatory approach to the Egyptian regime and never to open himself up to politics.

Beyond Egypt, things are different, but the importance of Salah as a positive role model still holds true. In the West, where populism, xenophobia, Islamophobia and fear of the Other prevail, where government policies create a hostile environment for refugees, immigrants and Arabs labelled as villains or terrorists, Salah, a North African Muslim, is winning hearts.

'If he's good enough for you he's good enough for me. If he scores another few, then I'll be Muslim too. If he's good enough for you he's good enough for me. Then sitting in the mosque is where I wanna be – Mo-Salah-la-la-la,' is sung by the Kop to the rhythm of Dodgy's 1994 hit 'Good Enough'. It may only be a chorus sung on the terraces but it is important. Because such simple, trivial things can help break down barriers, to help people change their minds about what is different, to bring together communities that live separately from one another in the same city. To provide a different image of Islam and bring trust to Muslims living in the West. '[Salah] is someone who embodies Islam's values and wears his faith on his sleeve,' Miqdaad Versi, assistant secretary general of the Muslim Council of Britain, tells the *New York Times*. 'He is the hero of the team. Liverpool, in particular, has rallied around him in a really positive way.

He is not the solution to Islamophobia, but he can play a major role.' Galib Khan, chairman of the Sheikh Abdullah Quilliam Mosque in Liverpool, adds that 'Mo has brought together children of all faiths and groups and colour and we are all proud of him. It brings fun to our lives. I think Mo has given us a gift that we will never forget.'

21

Never give up

He looked at the photo and told himself that what happened a year ago would not happen again, that things would be different this time. There would be no pain and no tears; this time they would walk out onto the pitch and win.

This is no mere hearsay or footballing legend. To motivate himself before the 2019 Champions League final, with UEFA's distinctive trophy up for grabs, Mohamed Salah did indeed look back at an image of Sergio Ramos's wrestling hold. Mo had been brought down hard on the Kiev pitch, injuring his shoulder and forcing him to come off just 30 minutes into the game. The bitterness of the defeat and its impact on his performance at the Russia World Cup later that summer still rankled. The Reds' number 11 swore he didn't spend too long looking at the picture, but said he needed to remember that moment. He was absolutely convinced that the second time would be something special, that they would come away with the biggest prize of all. And so it was. On 1 June 2019, Liverpool won the Champions League, beating Tottenham 2–0 in the final at Madrid's Wanda Metropolitano stadium. Football gave back to Salah what it had taken from him a year earlier and it did so in 22 seconds. The Reds were in possession from kick-off; their captain Jordan Henderson found Sadio Mané with a long ball down the left wing. Mané controlled the ball on the edge of the box, looked around him for an unmarked teammate and tried to cross to the other side of the Spurs penalty area. But Moussa Sissoko was standing stock still in front of him like a statue, his right arm stretching upwards. It stayed up and the ball struck him on his armpit, then on his arm. Damir Skomina, the Slovenian referee, was in no doubt. He felt no need to refer to VAR before pointing to the penalty spot. It fell to Mo to step up. A hop to the right and a short run-up before firing the ball with his left foot down the middle of the goal at waist height. Goal! The Egyptian slid on his knees towards the corner flag before being mobbed by his teammates. After the group hug he looked for a TV camera, brought two fingers up to either side of his nose, stuck his tongue out and smiled. A tribute, a planned celebration in honour of his daughter Makka.

It was already 1–0 after only one minute and 47 seconds of play, the third fastest goal in the history of European Cup finals. It was beaten only by goals scored by Real Madrid's Enrique Mateos in 1959, against Stade de Reims, and AC Milan's Paolo Maldini in Istanbul in 2005 in the historic final won by Rafa Benítez's Liverpool. Having gone 0–3 down in the first half, they came back to win on penalties.

The early goal determined the course of that final in the Wanda Metropolitano. There was no trace of the spirit that had seen Spurs knock out Ajax's fearsome kids. Jürgen Klopp's war machine wasn't running at its usual speed either. Mané and Salah had their handbrakes on. Both teams played completely through Henderson and Sissoko. The level of footballing spectacle was decidedly low: errors from both sides, missed passes and the tension turned up to the max. Liverpool were happy with their spoils and tried to manage them as best they could. There were very few chances: just two in the first half, when Alexander-Arnold hit the post and Lloris tipped a shot from Robertson over the crossbar. The

Reds conserved their energy in the second half as well: a shot from Milner – after an invitation from Salah – grazed the left post of Lloris's goal. For more than 70 minutes, Tottenham were convinced that sooner or later something would happen, that an equaliser would come. But it never did because, unlike a year earlier in Kiev, Liverpool had a goalkeeper in Alisson Becker who refused to let his attention wander. He was only tested by Spurs in the last quarter of an hour, when firstly Dele Alli, then Son, Lucas Moura and finally Eriksen posed any kind of serious threat. The Brazilian responded well. Up to that point, his greatest achievement had been a 60-metre pass to Salah. His opposite number, Lloris, didn't have all that much to do either, but in the 87th minute he was beaten for the second time. Milner swung in a corner from the right, but the Tottenham defence failed to clear the ball before it started bouncing around, eventually falling to Matip who somehow managed to send the ball towards Divock Origi. The super-sub scored with a low powerful left-footed shot into the corner; the poor French goalkeeper could do nothing about it. It was 2–0 and that was how it finished. Liverpool celebrated their sixth European Cup, the first trophy of the Jürgen Klopp era. Salah struggled to find any suitable adjectives: 'I have no words to describe such a glorious moment. It's great. The final of the Champions League, take a penalty, show the courage and win the trophy,' he said in a post-match interview before adding, with a smile, 'I prepared myself before the game. I scored a penalty to send Egypt to the World Cup after 28 years in the last minute so that tonight was easier.'

What is certain is that Momo, the Egyptian, had worked hard, believed and made plenty of sacrifices ever since he was a boy, spending hours travelling to and from Cairo, but in the end his dream had come true. He was only seven when he was first captivated watching the Champions League on television in Nagrig, imagining that one day he too would play in a match like this.

The triumph of 1 June 2019 brought an end to Salah's season for the Reds. But, despite the Champions League trophy and the Premier League Golden Boot, won for the second successive year (with 22 goals, tied with Sadio Mané and Pierre-Emerick Aubameyang), the 2018–19 season had not all been a bed of roses. It had got off to a great start. In the first league game of the season, 12 August 2018, the Pharaoh had opened the scoring in the 4–0 home win over West Ham. On 31 August, in Monte Carlo, he finished third in the UEFA Men's Player of the Year award, right behind Cristiano Ronaldo and Luka Modrić, the winner. The Croatian midfielder had won the Champions League with Real Madrid and led his country to the World Cup final in Russia. Also in Monte Carlo, he had a fleeting reunion with Sergio Ramos. After being named the best defender of the previous Champions League season, the Spaniard greeted Salah with a tap on the shoulder and a provocative grin. The Egyptian did not take it well and remained impassive, with his eyes fixed towards the stage.

Another awards ceremony came on 24 September in London, with the announcement of the Best FIFA Men's Player. The ranking remained unchanged from the UEFA awards a month earlier. Modrić won, followed by Cristiano, with Salah in third place. Mo was also the unexpected winner of the FIFA Puskás award for that goal in the snow at Everton on 10 December 2017. The final and long-awaited recognition of the year was the *France Football* Ballon d'Or, unveiled at a huge party in Paris on 3 December. Unfortunately, Momo failed to finish on the podium. He came sixth with 188 votes, compared with 753 for Luka Modrić, who had swept the board. He may not have won the French magazine award, but for the second year in a row Salah won the BBC prize for the best African Footballer of the Year. And, in Dakar, Senegal, he was elected the CAF Africa Player of the Year for the second consecutive time, beating his teammate Sadio Mané and Pierre-Emerick Aubameyang. The beauty was that his success and popularity went far beyond the sporting arena. Take *Time Magazine*, who named him one of the Hundred Most Influential People in the World alongside LeBron James, Mark Zuckerberg and Tiger Woods among others. John Oliver, a comedian and Liverpool fan, wrote in the magazine's profile of Mo: 'Salah is a better human being than he is a football player. Mo is an iconic figure for Egyptians, Scousers and Muslims the world over, and yet he always comes across as a humble, thoughtful, funny man who isn't taking any of this too seriously.' More recognition of his popularity came from the Pepsi commercial in which Leo Messi and Mohamed Salah face off for the last can left at a remote petrol station.

Beyond advertising, prizes and awards, the Reds' number 11 also had plenty to be pleased about on the pitch. At the end of the year, Liverpool were top of the Premier League table and seven points clear of Manchester City. They were unbeaten in the league and did not lose at Anfield at all in 2018. Jürgen Klopp's boys seemed well placed in the hunt for the holy grail of the Premier League. And that was not all: they had qualified second in their group behind Mbappé and Neymar's PSG and were in the last sixteen of the Champions League. Salah had contributed with three goals against Red Star Belgrade and Napoli. He had scored thirteen in the league. Everything seemed to be going well, but things can change quickly in football. On 3 January 2019 at the Etihad Stadium, the Citizens won 2–1 with goals from Kun Agüero and Sané. It was Liverpool's first league defeat and the break Pep Guardiola & Co needed. Instead of slipping ten points behind the leaders, they were now within four and threw themselves headlong into the race for the title. Over the months that followed, the Reds would not lose again but did chalk up four draws that would cost them dearly. It would allow City to move ahead of them on 3 March when the Reds drew away at Goodison Park in the Merseyside derby against Everton. It was a tiny advantage (71 points compared with Liverpool's 70), but it would stay that way until the end of the season. On 12 May, the 38th and final matchday of the Premier League Season, Manchester City came back to beat Brighton 4–1, taking them to 98 points, just one point ahead of Liverpool who won against Wolves. Pep Guardiola and the men in light blue, with a record-breaking second half of the season (eighteen wins and only one defeat against Newcastle), won their second consecutive title, the sixth in the club's history. Klopp and the men in red had to wave goodbye to the title. They hadn't won it for 29 years but had finally believed that it was within their grasp. All that remained was to focus on the Champions League final. The Reds had sealed their ticket to Madrid just five days earlier, on Tuesday 7 May, at Barcelona's expense and they had done so without Roberto Firmino or Mohamed Salah. Mo had taken a knock the previous Saturday at St James' Park in the Premier League game against Newcastle. At 2–2 Salah went up for a header when, Martin Dúbravka, the Magpies' keeper, came off the line to punch the ball and accidentally struck the Egyptian's head with his hip. Salah was down for several minutes. He received medical treatment and a decision was made to bring him off on a stretcher. Mo was in tears. He was diagnosed with concussion.

Salah ended up in the stands for the semi-final against Barcelona at Anfield. He was wearing a black T-shirt with the slogan 'Never Give Up' picked out in white. His teammates followed his instructions to the letter, never giving up and eventually proving that miracles do happen. No one, except perhaps Jürgen Klopp, believed the Reds could overturn the three goals they had conceded at the Camp Nou. Especially without their two top strikers. The statistics were stacked against Liverpool: only twice in the history of the European Cup had a team managed to overturn a 0–3 deficit after the first leg of a semi-final. Panathinaikos had managed it against Red Star in 1971, as had Barcelona against IFK Göteborg in 1986. Liverpool became the third team ever to pull off such an exploit, putting four past Barça, with two from Divock Origi and two from Georginio Wijnaldum. Anfield was delirious. Salah, with a beaming smile and his lucky shirt, ran onto the pitch to hug his teammates who had just given him the chance to play in another final. A final that, this time, would see him lift the Champions League cup on the pitch at the Wanda Metropolitano. A cup that Momo would fall asleep with in his arms on the flight back to Liverpool. A cup that put an end to controversy, rumours and more. There had been no lack of criticism of Salah in the spring. The number 11 wasn't scoring at the same rate as the previous year and had gone through a dry spell of six games, something that did not go unnoticed by journalists and commentators. Showing his irritation in a Sky Sports interview, Mo fired back: 'I didn't score for a couple of games, but there are some players who have the same number of goals as me. But people are saying those players are having the best season of their life. There are three or four players and no one talks about them – they say they have a good season and I'm the only one that has had a bad season.'

Also in April, rumours had surfaced in Spain that Momo was at loggerheads with Klopp to the extent that he had allegedly told the club he wanted to leave at the end of the season. Talk of Real Madrid, Zidane and Florentino Pérez, the president who always got what he wanted, refused to go away. The attention being paid to Mo by the Madrid club was said to be at the root of the dispute between the German manager and the Egyptian striker. The Champions League did much to calm the waters and dispel, at least for the moment, the spectre of a departure from Liverpool. Immediately after the final, Momo assured Movistar+ that it was not the time to discuss his future.

His season was not yet over; there was still the small matter of the 32nd Africa Cup of Nations. Egypt were the host nation and heavy favourites for the competition that began in Cairo on 21 June 2019. Directing operations from the bench, Javier Aguirre, the Mexican coach had selected Momo to wear the captain's armband. The hope of winning the continental title for the eighth time was great, but it soon faded. The Pharaohs finished top of Group A, with wins against Zimbabwe, the Democratic Republic of the Congo and Uganda. Salah scored twice. The Pharaohs were knocked out by South Africa in the last sixteen at Cairo's International Stadium on 6 July. No one expected a team that had qualified as the best of the third placed teams and only managed one win in Group B over Namibia to beat the host nation, yet Bafana Bafana got the win over the favourites, eliminating them from the tournament. Five minutes from the end, the South African midfield slotted a ball through on the right wing for Mothiba, who surged forward, offering up an assist to Thembinkosi Lorch. With only El Shenawy to beat, the yellow number 23 made no mistake. South Africa qualified for the quarter-finals with a 1–0 win. Mo cried bitter tears. His Senegalese teammate Sadio Mané would make the final but would also fail to lift the trophy which eventually went to Algeria. All that remained was to return to Europe and think about winning that elusive Premier League title.

22

Thirty years later

It was Saturday 28 April 1990. The end of a terrible year for Liverpool. Eleven months earlier, on 25 May 1989, they had seen the title slip from their grasp on the last day of the season in a winner takes all head-to-head with Arsenal at home at Anfield. Thanks to the 2–0 win sealed in the 92nd minute, the Gunners got the better of the Reds and won the First Division on goal difference. The match would go on to inspire the book *Fever Pitch* by Nick Hornby, a die-hard fan of the North London team. On 15 April 1989, at the Hillsborough Stadium in Sheffield, 96 Reds fans lost their lives during the FA Cup semi-final against Nottingham Forest. It was a terrible tragedy, the worst in English sporting history, coming less than five years after the Heysel Stadium disaster.

On 28 April 1990 Margaret Thatcher was living out the final months of her third term as Prime Minister of the United Kingdom. The Iron Lady was no football fan, but it was her government that kicked off a sea-change in British football in the wake of Heysel and Hillsborough. It would lead to the marginalisation of hooligans, the restructuring of stadiums and huge upheaval in the way games were enjoyed. Just as the Three Lions were preparing for the Italia 90 World Cup (which they would finish in fourth place), English football was undergoing great change.

The player manager Kenny Dalglish was on the bench for Liverpool at Anfield on Saturday 28 April 1990. On the pitch were Ian Rush, who had returned home after limited success in Italy with Juventus, John Barnes, the Jamaican who wore the number 10, and goalkeeper Bruce Grobbelaar, known for his 'spaghetti legs' in the 1984 European Cup final against Roma. Their opponents were Queens Park Rangers, tenth in the table. There were 37,758 spectators in the stands. Liverpool needed four points from their last three games to win the title. The match, which had the potential to be decisive, got off to a bad start. In the fourteenth minute, Roy Wegerle gave the Londoners the lead from a corner, before they nearly doubled their advantage through Colin Clarke, who hit the crossbar. Rush took care of restoring the Kop's confidence. He brought down a pass from the left from Steve Nicol with his chest and struck from an almost impossible angle to beat David Seaman. The winning goal came in the second half. On one of his raids down the wing, Nicol was taken down by Danny Maddix on the edge of the QPR area. The TV images would show that the foul was outside the box, but Robbie Hart, the referee, wasted no time thinking about it and awarded a penalty.

John Barnes, in a red shirt with Candy written across his chest, converted it. Anfield celebrated, but the fans did not yet dare to remove their headphones. The 37,000 plus fans were waiting for the result at Villa Park, where Aston Villa, second in the table, were drawing 3–3 against Norwich City. The game was not yet over. When the referee blew the final whistle at Anfield, the inevitable 'You'll Never Walk Alone' came over the speakers and Liverpool celebrated their eighteenth league title, the tenth in fifteen seasons. Thankfully, Aston Villa were kind enough not to break the deadlock in injury time. It would have been embarrassing, to say the least, during the Reds' lap of honour.

'Merseyside is at peace again. After the shame and remorse of Heysel and the personal grief of Hillsborough, there was real joy to behold for the first time in five years at Anfield on Saturday as Liverpool reclaimed the championship title and stepped towards Europe's beckoning arms,' wrote *The Times*.

On that joyful Saturday, no one would have imagined that the Reds would have to wait 30 years, 362 months or 11,016 days if you prefer, for their next league title. It would be unprecedented. Liverpool's next longest wait had been between their fourth title, won in 1923, and their fifth, in 1947, but the Second World War had, of course, led to the suspension of football between September 1939 and August 1946.

On 25 June 2020, when after five second-place finishes and five third-place finishes – after seeing top-of-the-table positions at Christmas vanish into thin air; after that slip by Steven Gerrard in 2014 and losing out by one measly point in 2018; after seeing their eternal rivals Manchester United collect thirteen titles; and after fearing that the 2019–20 season would be cancelled due to the coronavirus pandemic – finally, the nightmare was over. Liverpool were champions for the nineteenth time in their 128-year history, the first since the advent of the Premier League in 1992. Thirty years ago, confirmation of the win had come via transistor radio; this time the end of the curse was announced on live television.

On Thursday 25 June 2020, the night before, the Reds had beaten Crystal Palace 4–0 behind closed doors at Anfield, with goals from Alexander-Arnold, Salah, Fabinho and Mané. Mo said to Sky Sports after the game, 'I'm happy about the result and looking forward to the next two games. We had a great performance today and all the players were unbelievable. I think all the players are motivated, everyone is motivated in his way – but everyone is motivated to win.

Two points to go to win the league, it's great. Since I came here, I said I want to win the Premier League with the team. Maybe last year we had a chance to win it but Man City also performed really good [sic] and they won it. It's our time to win it and it's great. The city didn't win it for a long time, so it was the right time.'

It was time, time for Liverpool to take another step towards their first title in 30 years. They had amassed 86 points in 31 games and held a 23-point lead over second-placed Manchester City. The following day the Citizens had to beat Chelsea at Stamford Bridge if they wanted to postpone the Reds' coronation.

At 10.09 pm on Thursday 25 June, Jürgen Klopp and his players were in front of the TV at a central Liverpool hotel. In the dying moments of the game, the countdown began, punctuated by applause and hands trembling in the air; everyone was on their feet and then the shouting began. Chelsea's 2–1 win over Manchester City handed the title to the Reds who could no longer be caught, with seven games left to play. They hugged, smiled and shouted 'Campiones! Campiones!' The sky over Liverpool turned red. Around Anfield Road, despite the recommendations, bans and coronavirus lockdown, people had come to celebrate, letting off fireworks, smoke bombs and coloured flares, toasting in the street with alcohol brought from home.

Jürgen Klopp, in a Liverpool baseball cap and shirt, was emotional to the point of tears when he spoke to Sky Sports. 'This is a big moment; I have no real words. I am completely overwhelmed. I never thought I would feel like this! It's an incredible achievement by my players and it's a huge joy for me to coach them,' he said. He continued: 'I haven't waited 30 years, I have been here for four and a half years, but it is quite an incredible achievement, especially with the three-month break because nobody knew if we could go on. The boys have time together tonight. It's difficult out there still for a lot of people but tonight we couldn't hold back, we had to come together.' Live from the living-room of his home, King Kenny Dalglish, with a scarf around his neck, the manager who had won the last championship title and survived Covid-19, praised the work of the coach from Stuttgart: 'The last two years since Jürgen came in, it's been very, very positive all the way through. He's been fantastic and he epitomises everything that Liverpool Football Club stands for.' He ended by raising a glass to the win.

Mohamed Salah did not appear in front of the Sky Sports microphones, instead posting a photo on Instagram, smiling, wearing a club shirt and in the company of Alisson, Firmino, Fabinho and Lovren. 'Yes. It feels THAT good. I want to thank all our supporters watching us from all corners of the world. You made this possible for us and I hope we can keep bringing you the joy you deserve. Now they're gonna believe us.' Not quite painting the town red, but all that was left now was to party late into the night wearing a shirt that bore the words Champions 19–20 in gold: dancing and singing along to the soundtrack provided by Nightcrawlers' 'Push the Feeling On' and 'Show Me Love' by Robin S.

There was so much to celebrate: in addition to the end of the long wait for the title, the season had brought incredible results, plenty of satisfaction and some disappointments. It had been a very long season that had lasted almost a year after officially starting on Sunday 4 August 2019, with the final of the FA Community Shield. The Reds, Premier League runners-up, took on champions City at Wembley. It ended 1–1 after extra time, with goals from Sterling in the twelfth minute and an equaliser from Matip in the 77th. The trophy was decided on penalties. Claudio Bravo, the City keeper, saved Liverpool's second penalty taken by Georginio Wijnaldum. It was to be enough as the Citizens scored five out of five with their last one, taken by Gabriel Jesus, giving Pep Guardiola's boys the win. Salah managed ten shots on goal, hitting the outside edge of the post and missing a golden opportunity to make it 2–1 in the 93rd minute to finish off the game. One-on-one with Claudio Bravo, he tried to lob it over the keeper, but John Stones, the City's number 5, got in the way and the ball flew up into the air. Mo tried again, this time heading towards the open goal. It seemed like a guaranteed goal when Kyle Walker flew across with an overhead kick just under the crossbar, clearing the ball off the line. The first title of the season went to the team that had won the previous league title.

Ten days later Liverpool and Mo had the opportunity to make up for it. The European Super Cup was being played at the Vodafone Arena in Istanbul, a happy hunting ground for the Reds. Their opponents were Frank Lampard's Chelsea, who had won the Europa League in a London derby against Arsenal. The match referee Stéphanie Frappart, a 35-year-old Frenchwoman, became the first woman to referee a European final in men's football. It was 1–1 after 90 minutes. Olivier Giroud had given the Blues the lead before Mané, assisted by Firmino, equalised at the start of the second half.

Firmino and Mané combined once again to make it 2–1 to Liverpool and it looked as if it was all over, but Adrián, Liverpool's second goalkeeper, went in late on Abraham and Frappart awarded a penalty. Jorginho converted. The score was 2–2 after 120 minutes. Yet again, it would be decided from the spot. But unlike at Wembley in the Community Shield, the five Liverpool players called upon to take a kick (Firmino, Fabinho, Origi, Alexander-Arnold and Salah) made no mistake as Adrián redeemed himself by saving

Abraham's final penalty. In the Istanbul night, the Reds lifted their fourth European Super Cup and their first since 2005, when they had beaten CSKA Moscow.

Things were also going swimmingly in the league. The 28th Premier League season kicked off on 9 August. Liverpool played their first game at Anfield, beating Norwich City 4–1, with Salah scoring the second goal of the game. The Reds' winning streak lasted until the ninth match-day, 20 October, when they drew at Old Trafford, against Manchester United (1–1). They got back to winning ways the following week with a 2–1 win over Tottenham and they would not drop another point in until 29 February 2020, when Jürgen Klopp's boys suffered their first defeat of the season, going down 0–3 at Watford. In the middle of this run, Liverpool also won the FIFA Club World Cup for the first time in 127 years of history, with two hard-fought victories in Qatar. In the semi-final on 18 December 2019, the men in red beat the Mexicans from Monterrey 2–1. A stunning assist from Salah gave Naby Keïta the first goal and some hard work in the box to get past two opponents saw Roberto Firmino get the second in the 91st minute. The final came on 21 December against Flamengo. The Brazilians played a great game, shutting down the English and creating chances with Gabriel 'Gabigol' Barbosa. The Reds wasted theirs with Firmino who first found himself alone in front of goal but still fired the ball over the bar and later hit the post following a lovely move. Alisson distinguished himself, saving a diagonal shot from Gabigol, as did Diego Alves who stopped a long-range shot from Jordan Henderson. With the score locked at 0–0 after 90 minutes, once again, Liverpool were faced with extra time. The 99th minute saw a devastating counter-attack: with a long ball, Henderson found Mané, who passed to Firmino in the centre. The Brazilian tricked the defender with a body feint and struck the ball beyond the onrushing keeper. The final score was 1–0. Captain Henderson received the cup from Giovanni Infantino, FIFA President, before lifting it towards the sky. Liverpool were the 2019 World Champions. Mohamed Salah won the Golden Ball as the tournament's best player. It would be the first and only individual recognition of the season. Unlike the previous year, he failed to make the shortlist for the UEFA Men's Player of the Year, a trophy awarded to his teammate Virgil van Dijk. On 23 September 2019, at the gala for the best FIFA Men's Player held in Milan's Teatro della Scala, Salah finished fourth behind Leo Messi, Van Dijk and Cristiano Ronaldo. There was no shortage of controversy over the 26 points he received in the final ranking. According to the Egyptian Federation, the votes cast by its manager, the Pharaohs' captain and those of the country's media representatives were missing. Mo fell by one position to fifth in the final standings of the *France Football* Ballon d'Or 2019, finishing behind Sadio Mané, Cristiano Ronaldo, Van Dijk and Messi, who won his sixth Ballon d'Or. Mané also beat Salah in the Best African Player 2019 ranking on 7 January.

And then we come to the painful part of the season: elimination in the last sixteen of the Champions League. Late in the evening on 18 February 2020, Mohamed Salah walked through the mixed zone at the Wanda Metropolitano biting into an apple and responding to questions from the British press, who were looking for an explanation for the defending champions' defeat at the hands of Atlético Madrid, with a sharp 'No'. The number 11 walked right behind Van Dijk, who said of the game: 'It was a frustrating game. We knew it was going to be a battle and a very tough one because they are very organised. You have to be very patient and obviously the goal we conceded doesn't help. It's never nice to lose but we should be confident, not panicking. Obviously, we will take plenty of good things from this and do the bad things better.' It was true: Salah, who has an average of four shots per game, only managed to make himself dangerous on two occasions, while Mané and Firmino failed to worry Jan Oblak's goal.

Diego Simeone had come up with the perfect plan to pull the rug out from under Klopp's beloved Reds. Four minutes in Atlético took the lead. Fabinho struggled when a corner came in from the left and Saúl made no mistake from barely a yard out. From then on it was all defence, determination and hard work for Atlético as they waited for the right counter-attack. They executed it perfectly: in the remaining 86 minutes the Reds were unable to solve the problem, while the Colchoneros failed to finish off the game with an opportunity wasted by Álvaro Morata. Despite the defeat, Liverpool remained favourites to advance to the quarter-finals.

In the 43rd minute on 11 March at Anfield, Wijnaldum headed in a cross from Chamberlain to bring things back to level pegging. The script was the same in the second half: the Reds on the attack and the Colchoneros in defence, clinging on through Oblak whose gloves denied Salah, Chamberlain, Firmino, Alexander-Arnold and Wijnaldum. And when he did fail to stop an incoming shot, fortune smiled on him in the 66th minute when Robertson's powerful header hit the crossbar. Saving the Kop from desperation and his teammates from frustration, Firmino slotted home a simple tap-in in the 94th minute. Qualification seemed within their grasp. But in the 97th minute, Adrián made a huge mistake with a clearance that was picked up by João Félix and laid off to Marcos Llorente, who had come on in the second half for Diego Costa. He fired a right-footed shot just inside the far post. The former Real Madrid player was in great shape and provided an encore in the 105th minute: another right-footed strike from distance. A further goal from late substitute Morata in the 121st minute made it 2–4 on aggregate. The champions said goodbye to the Champions League and for Klopp's boys it was the fourth defeat in just a few weeks. On 18 February, Atlético had won 1–0; on 29 February, Watford won 3–0; and on 3 March, Chelsea had knocked them out of the FA Cup with a 2–0 win. There were warnings of the collapse of the red tide, but there was no time for anything else.

Two days later European football ground to a halt due to coronavirus. On 13 March, after Mikel Arteta, Callum Hudson-Odoi and staff from various clubs tested positive for Covid-19, the Premier League was suspended until 3 April. The plan was to return to the pitch on Saturday 4 April. But it was not to be: the Premier League would come back three months later. Three difficult months for everyone; three dark months of sickness, fear, silence, masks and uncertainty.

'People were saying cancel the league, some people were saying that you cannot play anymore. It was stress somehow and maybe everyone started to panic. It was tough as well to think that after such a long season, after that year, that they are going to cancel the Premier League again.' Salah told BBC Sport. He spent the lockdown at home with his family. 'I never had that time before so I was using it to enjoy it,' he explained. Glimpses of family life appeared on Instagram and in a Vodafone Egypt commercial. Mo playing in the garden and pool with his six-year-old daughter Makka; Mo talking to friends on his phone and iPad; Mo training on the green pitch behind his house; and Mo getting ready for Ramadan. A quiet life until the return of the Premier League. Liverpool played at 7pm on 21 June at Goodison

Park in a derby against Everton. One hundred and thirty days had passed since the last match played. Mohamed Salah remained on the bench, while the rustiness on the pitch, after such a long time, was apparent. The game ended in a limp goalless draw. They would have to wait another four days for Manchester City's defeat and the chance to celebrate the long-awaited title. And they would have to wait until 22 July, the penultimate day of the Premier League season and the Reds' final home game, for the title party, so that Jordan Henderson could lift a cup they had been waiting 30 years for after beating Chelsea 5–3. The cup was on display on the pitch at Anfield next to the Champions League, Super Cup and Club World Cup trophies. It was the setting for a family photo that Salah posted on Instagram on 25 July. Alongside him were Magi, his wife, and Makka. Smiling happily, Mo was holding a new arrival in his arms: Kayan, born on 8 February 2020.

Acknowledgements

We would like to thank the following people for their rec-
ollections and collaboration: Mohamed Afiz, Nacho Ares,
Walid Mamdouh, Annamaria Esposito, Francisco Carrión,
Auad Nagui el-Hoshy, Ali Abdel Tawab, Mohamed Abo
Hatab, Hamdy Nouh, Refaat Ragab, Saed el-Shishini,
Mohamed Abdelaziz, Mohamed Amer, Maher Anwar, Hany
Ramzy, Ahmed Ramadan, Mohamed Mansur, Mohamed
Bassyoni, Mohamed el-Bahnasy, Mohamed Eihofy, Mustafa
Helmy Eid, Ahmed Sayeyu, Um Ali, Mojtar el-Ashual,
Khaled Yousef el-Sharkawy, Mohamed Ismail, Tarek Omara,
Romain Beynié, Arnaud Bühler, Christophe Cerf, Bernard
Challandes, Roberto Crausaz, Damien Decrand, Ibrahim
el-Robi, Guillaume Faivre, Marco Fenni, Laurent Fontannaz,
Tim Guillemin, Maxime Gonalons, Clément Grenier,
Georg Heitz, Yoan Loche, Jérémy Manière, David Pelletier,
Stéphane Rinaldi, Mathieu Salamand, Patrick Sauteur,
Nicolas Soussan, Nestor Subiat, Mourad Tafer, Germano
Vailati, Javier Villagarcia, Sébastien Vuagnat and Murat
Yakin.

Thank you to Duncan Heath, Philip Cotterell, Michael
Sells, Laura Bennett, Ellen Conlon, Laure Merle d'Aubigné
and Roberto Dominguéz.

Thanks to Céline, Elvira, Lorenzo, Mathieu, Olmo and
Elisa for their support and valuable advice.